Bryan Norford

Bryan S Norford

GONE
—— WITH THE ——
SPIRIT

Tracking the Holy Spirit through the Bible

GONE WITH THE SPIRIT

Scripture taken from the Holy Bible, New International Version®. Copy-
right © 1973, 1978, 1984 International Bible Society. Used by permission
of Zondervan. All rights reserved.

ISBN: 978-1-77069-226-8

Printed in Canada.

Word Alive Press
131 Cordite Road, Winnipeg, MB R3W 1S1
www.wordalivepress.ca

Library and Archives Canada Cataloguing in Publication

Norford, Bryan, 1936-
    Gone with the spirit : tracking the Holy Spirit through the Bible /
Bryan Norford.

ISBN 978-1-77069-226-8

    1. Holy Spirit--Biblical teaching. I. Title.

BS680.H56N67 2011   231'.3   C2011-900977-3

Dedicated to our beloved grandchildren:
Jenny, Lee, Joshua, Dan, Dustin, Shawn and Luciano.

Contents

SOME HELPFUL THOUGHTS

What do the words "Holy Spirit" conjure up for you? Is it excitement at the experience you believe God has given you, or are you mystified by such claims? Is the Holy Spirit a positive presence in your life or simply a background force that energizes God's actions in the world? The title of this book, *Gone with the Spirit*, reflects usage in the Old and New Testament languages of the same word for "wind" and "spirit." But what does the title suggest to you? Does it imply those lost in wonder at the Spirit's friendly foray into their lives, or some who have apparently taken leave of their spiritual senses?

The Charismatic movement of the last century, a major phenomenon of church history, has created a divide between those claiming contemporary evidence of the New Testament Church's experience and sceptics who doubt similar activities occur today. Your answers to the forgoing questions will determine which approach you consider the most appropriate to your faith. Perhaps, like my experience, the force of Charismatic claims has undermined your own reason and experience and left you sitting uncomfortably on the fence. Although I grew up in and pastored

Pentecostal churches, I queried some contemporary practices of the New Testament Pentecostal experience. While Scripture identified much activity of the Holy Spirit that I saw demonstrated, how much was a legitimate expression? Which was the real thing or a counterfeit copy?

This book follows my previous book, *Guess Who's Coming to Reign: Jesus Talks about His Return*, written in a similar format. The purpose for that book was to give an overview of a subject that has become clouded by speculation and fiction, to the point where many have given up study of the subject. *Gone with the Spirit* attempts to provide an overview of the contentious and poorly understood person and work of the Holy Spirit. As in my previous book, I have deliberately kept sections short for use as a study guide, and to aid finding information from a particular part of the Bible. Scripture references deliberately interrupt the text to encourage reading them, and Scriptures at the head of most sections provide helpful reading to establish contextual setting for the events. In addition, each section provides material for a weekly discussion in group study.

A lifetime of study and teaching on the subject lies behind this small book, and I pray it may help you to a secure understanding of the issue. The Bible gives perspective that goes beyond blinkered teaching based on sporadic references. It provides a broad-based view of the actions of the Holy Spirit over millennia that will help identify his work today.

Terminology

I want you to have a clear understanding of the terminology I have used. The title "Evangelical" defines the Christian group that considers the Bible as God's inspired and inerrant message to us in the original written documents. Modern translations of the Bible endeavour to reproduce those original documents as accurately as possible. "Pentecostals" and "Charismatics" both belong to this group, but differ in their understanding of the work of the Holy Spirit. The charismatic stance on the issue now defines a separate category within evangelicalism.

There are some distinctions between Pentecostals and Charismatics. Pentecostals were the first to identify the modern activity of the Holy Spirit about the beginning of the twentieth century. Unable to remain in their parent churches due to harassment, they separated, and new Pentecostal denominations emerged. The Charismatic movement, following similar experiences and ideas, began in the sixties, but unlike Pentecostals, grew in groups that generally remained in their traditional churches. Belief in the modern work of the Spirit, as described in the New Testament Church, is common to both groups.

References cited are from The New International Version (NIV) of the Bible. The NIV capitalizes the initial letters designating the Holy Spirit to distinguish it from other uses of the word *spirit*; for example, used as a synonym for "attitude." In particular, lower case use of the initial letter for *spirit* identifies its use for other created beings such as angels, evil and lying spirits. Note the different terms used in the Bible for the Holy Spirit's activity on people: take from, put upon, rest upon, give, have, baptize, and fill, among other terms. They all describe the similar effect of the Spirit uniting with people in both Old and New Testaments.

You may find it helpful to note that the names of Messiah and Christ are interchangeable. "Messiah" is a transliteration from the Hebrew in the Old Testament, and "Christ" from the Greek in the New; but they both have the same meaning: "The Anointed One."

Finally, there is a difference in meaning between the names God and Lord. God, *Elohim* in Hebrew, is the creator of the universe, the universal King of creation, and to whom all inhabitants of the earth are accountable. Lord, *Yahweh* in Hebrew, printed in capitals as "LORD" in the Old Testament, is a sort of shorthand for the God of Abraham, Isaac and Jacob, designating his particular role as the covenant God of Israel. The Bible sometimes uses these titles interchangeably. The cry "Jesus is Lord," in the New Testament is a proclamation that Jesus is the covenant Lord of the Old Testament and of his people, not only for the Jew but also for all those he calls to himself.

PART ONE

PRIOR CONSIDERATIONS

1

Preliminary Perspectives

Personal

After a teaching session during my pastorate of a Pentecostal church several years ago, an enthusiastic member asked, "Well, where is the Spirit in all this?" He assumed a message without a liberal sprinkling of references to the Holy Spirit—especially in a Pentecostal church—was not authentic. The simple answer was, "Well, the Holy Spirit wrote the Word we've been discussing."

However, the exchange raised the possibility of constructing a message, even a series of messages, without any reference to the Holy Spirit. After all, references to the Spirit are frequent through the Bible; considerably more so in the New Testament. Yet often the preached message sounds as if the Holy Spirit is in the background pulling strings, but not directly relevant to what is happening centre stage.

The Bible is the primary source for our belief, and Evangelical Christian groups accept that the Holy Spirit inspired its authors, creating God's Word for us. Thus, the Bible is the unique basis for proclamation of the Gospel and learning of the person and work of the Holy Spirit; no other source can supplant it. But it is the Spirit who gives the Word life. Without his illumination, the Word may be interpreted according to our fallen wisdom and desires. Many pseudo-Christian sects who distort the Word for personal ends make the point.

Yet, indulgence in the Spirit-given gifts without the stabilizing instruction of the Word may develop into mere spiritism. The Word's guidance is necessary to distinguish the true voice of the Spirit from other misleading spirits, or human spiritual usurpers seeking to manipulate or control others for their own purposes. The Montanist movement of the second century began as a revived move of the Spirit, but descended into error when personal prophecies usurped the authority of Scripture. Sufficient tragedies of our own time demonstrate the dangers of seeking spiritual inspiration divorced from the Word—the tragedy of Jonestown a typical example. Jim Jones, originally a Pentecostal pastor, persuaded his church to relocate to Guyana. There, at his command, over 900 members died of self-administered cyanide poisoning in an event termed "revolutionary suicide."

Like two wings of a bird, Word and the Spirit are both necessary, either one without the other creates a recipe for distortion and deception. Despite this obvious truth, Charismatics and Evangelicals have viewed each other with suspicion and, while not denying some relevance of the other, each has tended to lean more to one side to avoid perceived mistakes of the other.

Charismatics are apprehensive of a sterile interpretation of the word, while Evangelicals fear disruption by those deceptively claiming to be the Spirit's messenger.

Having spent much of my life in Pentecostal and Charismatic circles, I am aware of both the strengths and weaknesses of the movement. But close association with Evangelicals and their writings has also given me insight into their response to Charismatic claims. This book presents an overview of the work of the Holy Spirit through the Bible of sufficient breadth that it may provide a balanced approach between Charismatic and Evangelical understanding.

HISTORICAL

While there have been several outbreaks of Charismatic fervour during the history of the Church, nothing has matched the spread of the Charismatic Movement in the twentieth century. But what may seem normal today was neither generally experienced nor understood a hundred years ago. Vinson Synan, in his historical record, *The Century of the Holy Spirit*, records growth of the combined Pentecostal and Charismatic Movement from one million adherents in 1901 to 500 million worldwide by 2001. This group is now the second largest identifiable group in Christendom after the Catholic Church. Furthermore, it has had a major impact upon non-charismatic worship in more traditional fellowships, encouraging more individual expression and informal services in addition to the liturgical. The movement's influence and eventual endorsement in the Catholic Church has added breadth to its impact.

Differing interpretations of Holy Spirit theology by Luke and Paul is a source of disagreement between Charismatic and Evangelical thinking. Charismatics have concentrated mostly on Luke's accounts of the Spirit's miraculous activity in his Gospel and Acts, while Evangelicals prefer Paul's everyday teaching on the Spirit's work. As a result, the primary division between these groups is the miraculous ministry of the Spirit, widely practiced by Charismatics, but viewed with suspicion by Evangelicals. Some extreme Charismatic behaviour may raise the charge that the Holy Spirit is being blamed or credited for actions he has nothing to do with. On the other hand, some extreme Evangelicals could be in danger of crediting Satan with the Spirit's work.

There are risks in each position without recognizing the validity of the other. Do not be drawn into distortions that have interfered with the Spirit's work. Evangelicals have rightly claimed that some in the Charismatic movement base their interpretation of Scripture on personal experience, reading into the text what their experience may imply. This makes experience the arbiter of Scripture rather than the reverse. Charismatics accuse Evangelicals of missing a major move of God through his Spirit and of downplaying the possibility of miraculous signs of the Holy Spirit in the contemporary Church. Some Charismatics have developed an elitist approach to those who disagree with them. According to them, those who bypass the Spirit's charismatic work have apparently forfeited God's fullness and so lead less effective spiritual lives.

Taking a position at the extreme end of the evangelical position, "Cessationists," as their name suggests, claim the gifts of the Spirit *ceased* when the New Testament was complete. Typically, they claim 1 Corinthians 13:8–10 indicates that tongues, prophecies, and knowledge will pass away "when perfection comes." Here, "perfection" is considered completion of the New Testament; thus the gifts that provided interim spiritual knowledge are no longer required. This interpretation is unlikely as the context of verse 12 indicates the perfect will come when "we shall see face to face," which refers to the final reunion with our Lord. By dismissing contemporary manifestations of the Spirit's work, better understanding of the Spirit's influence in today's Church is restricted.

In my view, the difference between Charismatics and Evangelicals is primarily a disagreement over what is relevant for Holy Spirit activity today, rather than dismissal of related texts. There is general agreement on a basic statement of faith. Both are brothers and sisters in Christ and deserve respect as such. Neither has a monopoly on the faith, and as the Charismatic movement has recently matured, there is evidence of greater cooperation between Charismatics and Evangelicals.

For example, the Alpha movement led by Nicky Gumbel which has had such a great impact across the denominational spectrum, has its roots in the charismatic Anglican Church. This has led the more traditional churches, which embrace the Alpha movement and its clarifying presentation of the Gospel, to consider and cautiously adapt the "Holy Spirit Weekend" included in the program.

2

WHO IS THE
HOLY SPIRIT?

Scripture does not depict the Holy Spirit as some sort of ghost or disembodied Christ, but as a separate being having all the attributes of God and displaying individual personality. The Christian Church agreed on the deity of Holy Spirit by the third century, after the demise of the Arian and Macedonian heresies. Arius assumed one God, the Father, but that Jesus and the Holy Spirit were created beings. Macedonius tried the intermediate position that Jesus was divine with the Father, but the Spirit was a created being.

The final belief in the Trinitarian formula recognizing Father, Son and Holy Spirit as equally divine has been the position of the Church since then to the present. Believing anything less about the Holy Spirit, demotes him and restrict his actions among humanity. Furthermore, a created Holy Spirit would not have the power or authority to fulfill his mission portrayed in Scripture.

DEITY OF THE HOLY SPIRIT

God is one in his essential being, but exists in three individual persons in such a way that the divine essence is wholly in each person. Simply put, whatever spiritual or other substance God is made of, all three share in that substance. This formula is not easy to understand, and individual Christian recognition and maintenance of it—with some exceptions—rather than seeking a simpler principle, is mute testimony to its pervading truth. The difficulty many have in assimilating the idea of one God in three Persons, has generated Islam, Mormonism and Jehovah's Witnesses among others, who demote Christ or the Holy Spirit or both, to created beings. Remember, the demotion of Jesus Christ to less than divine status defines pseudo Christian groups.

Several Scriptures give the Holy Spirit equal status with the Father and the Son. If you have been baptised, you may recall the formula for baptism, "in the name of the Father and of the Son and of the Holy Spirit," Matthew 28:19. This parallels the baptism of Jesus, Matthew 3:16–17, where all three members of the Trinity are present and active. In 1 Corinthians chapter 12, the Holy Spirit is given the similar status to the Lord Jesus, verse 3, and in verse 11 is revealed as equivalent to God himself, as he distributes spiritual gifts. The opening address of Peter's first letter lists the three persons of the Trinity: the Father, the Spirit and Jesus Christ, and in his first sermon, Peter noted the combined actions of the Trinity in the process of Salvation, Acts 2:32–33. The benediction closing Paul's second letter to the Corinthians includes the three members of the Trinity, "May the grace of the Lord Jesus Christ, and the love of God, and the fellowship of the Holy Spirit be with you all." 2 Corinthians 13:14.

While the Holy Spirit listed with the Father and the Son does not necessarily signify his deity, it is corroborating evidence that builds on divine names attributed him. In Acts 5:3–4, lying to the Holy Spirit is the equivalent of lying to God. In the Old Testament, the temple was the dwelling place of God. In the New Testament, God lives in the Christian and it is the Holy Spirit as God who indwells the believer.

In 2 Peter 1:20–21, Peter describes the Holy Spirit as the One who inspired the writers of Scripture. Paul, in his second letter to Timothy, claims all Scripture is *theopneustos,* that is, "God-breathed," 3:16. Tfhe word *theopneustos* is a combination of *theos*, "God," and *pneuma*, "breath" or "spirit." Thus, Paul designates the Holy Spirit as the Breath of God, inspiring the sacred writings. Compare this to the wordplay of "wind" and "Spirit" by Jesus in John 3:8.

In addition, Scripture credits him with divine attributes. He is omnipresent, Psalm 139:7–12, and he is omniscient, Isaiah 40:13, where the alternate reading is Spirit of the LORD; compare this with 1 Corinthians 2:10–11. The Holy Spirit is omnipotent, displaying his power as he will, Romans 15:18–19 and 1 Corinthians 12:11. Beyond these, the book of Hebrews refers to the Holy Spirit as "the eternal Spirit," 9:14, and Paul claims, "The Lord is the Spirit," 2 Corinthians 3:17.

Finally, the Holy Spirit performs divine works. He is co-Creator of the universe, Genesis 1:2 and of humankind, Job 33:4. He re-creates, Psalm 104:29–30, and brings new birth, John 3:5–6 and Titus 3:5. Paul proclaimed the Holy Spirit, who raised Jesus from the dead and indwells all believers, as the one who will bring us life beyond the grave, Romans 8:11.

PERSONALITY OF THE HOLY SPIRIT

Actions required for creation, design, problem solving and directing moral choice, are functions of personality. Those characteristics, which humans experience as a person created in the Image of God, also define the Holy Spirit as a person. Isaiah's sevenfold description of the Holy Spirit in 11:2, gives us an overview of the personality traits he possesses. Of prime importance, he is the Spirit of the LORD, and in so being, embraces the entire essence of God. The Holy Spirit displays *wisdom*, which reveals the nature of God and provides a pattern of holy, ethical life. He has *understanding* that discerns between good and evil. His faculty of *counsel* is the ability to plan strategy, and he has the *power* to fulfill the plan. It is not merely raw power but power tempered with justice and righteousness. He has intimate *knowledge* of God that draws love and obedience from his people, and he delights "in the *fear of the LORD*," that promotes reverence, awe and piety.

The Holy Spirit also demonstrates traits of personality familiar in human life: intellect, will, and emotions. He uses intellect to "search the deep things of God," 1 Corinthians 2:10, while he expresses his will in the distribution of spiritual gifts, as "he gives them to each one, just as he determines," 1 Corinthians 12:11. The Spirit's emotions are revealed in his love, Romans 15:30, and in his grief, Isaiah 63:10, Ephesians 4:30, when his influence is refused, 1 Thessalonians 5:19–20.

In the New Testament, John uses the masculine personal

pronoun *ekeinos,* referring to the Holy Spirit, 12 times in Chapter 16. Occasional uses of "it" for the Holy Spirit in the New Testament occur where it agrees with the neuter noun *pneuma.*

You might not consider the foregoing terms defining the deity and personality of the Holy Spirit conclusive evidence. However, the experience, conviction, and pointers left by the writers of Scripture leave us sufficient certainty of the Holy Spirit's divinity, that it has become the mainstay of Christian belief. Perhaps less obvious in the Old Testament, but clear in the New, all members of the Trinity participated in extending to us that marvellous salvation and life with Christ that is our privilege and joy. The Father sent the Son to die for us, and we are born anew into the Kingdom by the Spirit.

Facets of the Spirit's Ministry

There is a qualitative difference between his ongoing direction and revelation in the individual lives of God's people and his visible, miraculous intervention recorded throughout Scripture. Scripture given as "men spoke from God as they were carried along by the Holy Spirit," 2 Peter 1:21, and the interpretation of dreams by Joseph and Daniel demonstrate the former. By contrast, raising the dead by Elijah and Elisha and the Spirit's descent upon the disciples in Acts chapter 2 are examples of the Spirit's charismatic work. There may be instances where the dividing line is blurred; the enabling by God's Spirit of Bezalel to perform functions similar to natural talents, comes to mind.

Two clear differences also emerge in the action of the Holy Spirit upon individuals. First, the Spirit indwells a person on a permanent basis, as we will see in Joseph, David, and the believers in the New Testament after Pentecost. But we will note that King Saul had this "permanence" terminated and the Holy Spirit withdrew from Samson for a period. However, there is no record of the Spirit leaving those filled in this manner in the New Testament. It is from this continuous indwelling of the Spirit that guidance and direction for life generally come. In this book, I will generally refer to such action of the Spirit as "investment."

Second, the Holy Spirit fills individuals in a one-time action to provide the recipient power or strength for a particular challenge. Ezekiel, in the Old Testament, is a prime example as the Spirit took him to several locations for instruction and revelation. Although Peter was initially filled by the Spirit on the Day of Pentecost, the Holy Spirit filled Peter again as he faced the persecuting Sanhedrin. Several incidents in Acts repeat similar experiences. I have used the word "empowering" for this specific recurring action of the Holy Spirit.

Finally, the continuing incidental mention of the work of the Spirit within God's work, suggests that the Holy Spirit is working as God far more often than the statistics suggest. As that may be, this book generally stays with the direct references to the Holy Spirit to specifically identify evidence of his person and work.

These ideas may be familiar to you. You may have felt the Spirit's empowering or indwelling as a specific experience, following the pattern of those from Scripture we have mentioned. It has been a meaningful and strengthening event in your life and assisted in establishing your faith. On the other hand, you may have been a Christian for many years, yet not experienced anything like this. It has left you questioning Scripture and sceptical of those claiming such experiences. However, as we shall find,

Who is the Holy Spirit?

God's Spirit comes to indwell all believers, whether in an overwhelming explosion of power, a silent invasion by faith, or some experience in between. Given his way, the Spirit will guide, direct and strengthen each of us throughout life, whatever our experience of him.

PART TWO

THE OLD TESTAMENT

3
SETTING THE STAGE

READ: Genesis 1:1–2; 6:1–7; 41:33–40

References to the Holy Spirit occur from Genesis to Revelation. The New Testament, although only a quarter the length of the Old Testament by volume, contains the most references to the Holy Spirit found in the complete Bible. Many of today's Pentecostal and Charismatic believers rely heavily on the New Testament, often on a small portion of New Testament references, for understanding the work of the Holy Spirit. However, over ninety references to him in the Old Testament provide a foundation for understanding his work.

THE PUNCTUATED CHARISMATIC WORK OF THE SPIRIT

We have noted, and will continue to find, the experience of the Holy Spirit varies from person to person, yet his presence and influence is consistent in all Christians. Similarly, although the Spirit's charismatic work is not continuous, he works continually throughout history influencing the lives of people and nations. His miraculous intervention in the life of Israel is generally restricted to times of challenge, especially noticeable in the Old Testament as it covers several millennia. The following list of approximate dates gives an indication of the punctuated experiences of the Holy Spirit's visible intervention in the life of Israel. These dates are all B.C.

- 1500–1400: Moses and Joshua, at the founding of the nation of Israel.

- 1250–1150: Gideon, Jephthah and Samson, during apostasy at the time of the Judges.

- 1100–1000: Saul and David, at the founding of the Kingdom of Israel.

- 875–824: Elijah and Elisha, at Israel's peak apostasy during the reign of Ahab.

- 600–500: The Period of the Exile.

We will go into more detail of the Holy Spirit's work in these periods later in the book. While we read of the Holy Spirit's activity in between these periods, manifestations of the miraculous generally appear within them. It sets the stage for a better understanding of the history of the Holy Spirit during the Church age up to this time. This book, concerned with the work of the Holy Spirit in Scripture, will not refer to history subsequent to the New Testament, but the following dates will serve to note the punctuated charismatic work of the Holy Spirit since the Early Church similar to the Old Testament record. The dates are all A.D.

- 30–100: Founding of the New Testament Church.

- 150–250: The Montanist Movement.

- 550–604: Bishop Gregory and Pope Gregory the Great record supernatural happenings.

- 1150: Beginning of the Waldensians.

- 1550: Widespread supernatural activity within the Reformed Church in France.

- 1700–1900: Escalating widespread revivals throughout the world.

- 1900–2000: Founding and spreading of the Charismatic experience worldwide.

Noticeable in this list is the explosion of Holy Spirit activity during the last century. This major movement of the Spirit underlines the importance for ensuring a scriptural understanding of the person and work of the Holy Spirit.

The Old Testament sets the stage for the Spirit's work in the book of Genesis. The three references to the Holy Spirit in Genesis each reflect a facet of his work among humankind.

THE SPIRIT'S CREATIVE WORK

We have already addressed the deity of the Holy Spirit, but his inclusion in the second verse of the Bible as co-Creator in the creation story is a clear pointer to his status within the Trinity. "Now the earth was formless and empty, darkness was over the surface of the deep, and the Spirit of God was hovering over the waters," Genesis 1:2. Compare this with John's introduction to his Gospel as he repeats the first three words of Genesis, "In the beginning . . . ."

John's deliberate ploy here is to introduce Jesus also as co-Creator, establishing Jesus' place in the Trinity. The theme of Christ as co-Creator and Sustainer occurs again in Colossians 1:15–18. Thus the Bible, as it introduces Jesus in the New Testament, includes him as co-Creator with the Holy Spirit and a member of the Trinity.

God refers to himself in the plural in Genesis 1:26, "Let *us* make man in *our* image." (my emphasis). Furthermore, the name for God in the Hebrew Old Testament, *Elohim*, is the plural of *El,* which is the generic word for "god." Thus, the word *Elohim* can certainly be translated "gods," the context determining that option, or the more common translation "God," incorporating the idea of the Trinity. We will discuss this differing understanding further in reviewing the final Holy Spirit reference in Genesis.

But for our immediate purpose, Genesis 1:2 designates the initial operation of the Holy Spirit as Creator, recognized by Job, 33:4 and the Psalmist, 104:30. Miracles of the widow's jar of oil and the raising of the Shunamite's son are typical of the Spirit's creative work through Elijah and Elisha. Similar reports through the Old Testament speak of the continuing creative work of the Holy Spirit.

However, it is in the New Testament that his creative work comes to prominence. Probably the most obvious is the creative work of producing a body for Jesus within the womb of the Virgin Mary. But the re-creative work of the Spirit in the hearts of New Testament believers is the main emphasis. New birth comes via the Spirit, John 3:5–8, Titus 3:5; regeneration is by the Spirit, 1 Corinthians 6:11, which persuaded Paul to declare that Christians are a new creation in Christ, 2 Corinthians 5:17.

The Spirit's Convicting Work

We find reference to the Spirit's convicting work in Genesis 6:1–8. Conviction of sin in light of Christ's righteousness leads to the realization of our need and his sufficiency. Having experienced this work of the Spirit, you will understand the Spirit striving with people to leave their wicked ways prior to the flood. Thus, Genesis introduces the convicting work of the Holy Spirit upon humanity. The most evident work of the Holy Spirit in this regard is the inspiration of the Bible as the Word of God, demonstrating God's desire to bring men and women to repentance and reconciliation with him. John specifically records Jesus' discussion of the convicting work of the Spirit in chapter 16 of his Gospel, which we explore later.

It is noteworthy that conviction in the Bible speaks primarily of convincing the minds of men and women of the truth. That truth is not just confirming the existence of God, but also his plan and power to restore humanity to himself through Jesus Christ. As Paul states:

> What may be known about God is plain to them, because God has made it plain to them. For since the creation of the world God's invisible qualities—his eternal power and divine nature—have been clearly seen, being understood from what has been made, so that men are without excuse. (Romans 1:19–20)

However, many will accept neither the evidence of nature nor the witness of the Spirit concerning God's requirements set out in the law. Paul points out that this law, which God gave in verbal form to the Hebrews, he also wrote on the hearts of men, Romans 2:14–15. Upon rejection of that law, the convicting work of the Spirit will not be to convince for repentance, but to convict for judgment. As Paul says later in Romans, "Now we know that whatever the law says, it says to those who are under the law, so that every mouth may be silenced and the whole world held accountable to God," Romans 3:19.

THE INDWELLING SPIRIT

The final reference to the Spirit in Genesis 41:38, speaks of the indwelling Spirit in Joseph. If you are among those that did not experience a direct manifestation of the Spirit's arrival in your life, take heart: there is no record that Joseph did either. But the presence of the Spirit was nevertheless evident to others. Pharaoh, upon hearing Joseph's interpretation of his dreams, set Joseph up as his surrogate in all matters of state. Pharaoh explained his reasoning: "Can we find anyone like this man, one in whom is the spirit of God?" Then Pharaoh said to Joseph, "Since God (or the gods) has made all this known to you, there is no one so discerning and wise as you. You shall be in charge of my palace, and all my people are to submit to your orders. Only with respect to the throne will I be greater than you," Genesis 41:38–40.

The NIV alternative reading for verse 38 is "spirit of the gods." Our previous discussion regarding the translation of *Elohim*—either "God" or "gods"—provides us with the reason for this alternative. In fact, as we review the situation from the different perspectives of Pharaoh and Joseph, it is reasonable to recognize both translations as relevant. It was logical for Pharaoh to speak of gods in the plural because he was the ruler of a polytheistic nation. However, as Joseph worshipped the one true God, he recognised that Pharaoh's "spirit of the gods" referred to the Spirit of the one God indwelling him.

It is relevant to note that in the Old Testament the Spirit indwelt specific individuals. While we will look at this in more detail as we progress through the Bible, we will observe through the Old Testament that those called by God for specific service received the Spirit's investment or empowering. However, as a result of the Spirit's descent and empowering on the Day of Pentecost, the Holy Spirit indwells all Christians, John 14:17, Romans 8:9–11. Christians are now his temple or dwelling place, both individually, 1 Corinthians 6:19, and corporately, 2 Corinthians 6:16. The same Spirit that invested himself in Joseph's life also indwells us in response to our commitment to Christ.

What is remarkable about the accounts of the Spirit's work in Genesis is the accuracy of its portrayal compared with the operation of the Holy Spirit throughout the rest of the Bible. As the Holy Spirit is the author of Scripture through many writers, this opening description of his work is consistent with future revelations of the Holy Spirit.

4

THE DESERT
WANDERINGS

READ: Exodus 31:1–6; Numbers 11:10–30;
23:1–30 and 24:1–25

If you are familiar with the manifestation of the Spirit, the experiences recorded here, particularly the prophesying of those called to leadership, will be meaningful. But those of you more familiar with the quiet outworking of the Spirit in life will also find meaning in Bezalel and his associates. The gifts given them were silent evidence of the Spirit's empowering.

These aspects of the Holy Spirit's enabling occur in the desert wanderings of the Israelites. Exodus to Deuteronomy report craftsmanship, leadership, and prophecy during the journey. As we noted previously, the Old Testament records the anointing or filling by the Holy Spirit of specific people appointed for leadership or specific tasks. The people that left Egypt as a rabble of slaves were now developing into a nation, assisted by the Holy Spirit's intervention recorded in the Pentateuch. These references relate to the gifting and anointing work of the Holy Spirit.

CRAFTSMANSHIP

The first references record the enabling for craftsmanship. In parallel passages, Exodus 31:1–6 and 35:30–35, Bezalel is filled with the Holy Spirit "to make artistic designs for work in gold, silver and bronze, to cut and set stones, to work in wood, and to engage in all kinds of craftsmanship." In addition, the Spirit empowered others with the skill necessary to work and embroider fabrics.

While these gifts recognize the creative work of the Spirit, it raises the issue whether genetically acquired talents and Spirit-empowered ones are identical. Is the Spirit using or enhancing natural talents, or creating new ones in the individual? It is clear from Genesis 4:19–22 that the skills of farming, music and craftsmanship are naturally found in earth's human inhabitants. These three suggest many other talents developed from agriculture, art and artisanship, and which we experience in others and ourselves.

The difference between natural talents and Spirit-enabled gifts lies in their purpose, more than their function. Whether in the Old or New Testaments, the Holy Spirit's enabling is for spiritual development of either individuals or the community as a whole. We may conclude that the Spirit may use or enhance natural talents, or provide abilities not resident in the individual to accomplish his purpose. We may see inspiration in the work of those so filled, as with Bezalel, but also see in others spiritual insight and revelation that would not be possible from the fallen nature of our human understanding. In this sense, the operation of these gifts may often be a miraculous work of the Spirit.

This incident may also reveal the tip of a wider work—beyond the charismatic—of the Holy Spirit in the inspiration of art and industry. The word "inspiration" itself indicates a source inspired (breathed in) from some spirit. Without defining the limits of Spirit inspiration, we are aware of inspired music in Handel's Messiah and inspired art in the ceiling of the Sistine Chapel. We cannot restrict the Holy Spirit's work to Christians alone, as he will speak to humanity and bring conviction on whomever he will.

Furthermore, like Bezalel, Christians are engaged in a vocation; that is, a calling, not an occupation. When we are engaged in constructive pursuits for society, we are giving that "cup of cold water" to improve the well-being of those around us. The enabling of workers for the tabernacle of Moses' time is a visible part of the Spirit's work ensuring that God's kingdom will come and his "will be done on earth as it is in heaven." Matthew 6:10.

Leadership

The story of Moses and the elders in Numbers 11:10–29 describes the visible enabling of the Holy Spirit for leadership, the context assuming the Holy Spirit had already anointed Moses for leadership of God's people. Moses felt that the burden God imposed on him was too great, yet he failed to share the burden with others. Spirit anointing does not inoculate us from our human failings. But the erratic behaviour of the Israelites and the problems it created are recalled by the Psalmist, 106:32–33, as the people rebelled, not against Moses, but against the Spirit of God.

Seventy men who were "leaders and officials among the people," Numbers 11:16, were set apart to assist Moses in serving the people. God shared the same Spirit that enabled Moses with them and they prophesied. This prophesying does not appear predictive in any sense; there is no record of the content of the prophecy. Its function seems purely to signify to God's people his appointment of these men for service, and in this sense, it appeared to serve a similar function to tongues recorded in Acts chapter 2 of the New Testament.

This is the first example in the Bible identifying the anointing of the Spirit by some form of ecstatic utterance. But why does there not appear to be any reaction by the recipients or viewers to an *unnatural* phenomenon. An unexpected *natural* event can cause consternation, even panic, but these people seemed unfazed. It may be that similar events had occurred in the past but were not recorded. Either way, this occasion clearly institutes the intrusion of the Holy Spirit into the life of his people.

The amusing incident of Eldad and Medad is a story that, with variations, is similar to those in contemporary Christian circles who box God into traditional settings. It seems that spiritual experiences in Israel were set within certain spiritual locations; in this case at the Tent of Meeting where God met with Moses. Eldad and Medad were prophesying in the camp among the people, and a local telltale ran to tell Moses of this infraction. Even Joshua, in the enthusiasm of his youth, called on Moses to stop them.

Moses' reply was both classic and prophetic. Rather than restricting God's touch to a few, Moses wished it on all God's people. He had no desire to be one of a privileged few, but wanted what he and the elders had experienced for all. His utterance was certainly prophetic, whether he realized or not, for the time came when God's Spirit did fall upon all his people, beginning at the day of Pentecost.

When the time came for Moses to die, Moses called on God for a replacement to look after the people of Israel. God chose Joshua, "a man in whom is the Spirit," Numbers 27:18. Deuteronomy 34:9 reminds us, "Joshua, son of Nun, was filled with the Spirit of wisdom because Moses had laid his hands on him." This is not only a reminder of the indwelling function of the Spirit, but also a reference to a specific gift, that of wisdom. As we progress through Scripture, both the Old and New Testaments identify gifts of the Spirit more frequently.

Prophecy

One approach to prophetic utterance has been to separate "foretelling," from "forthtelling." Foretelling is the ability to predict future events, which may or may not be clear to the prophet or observer. Most people understand that definition. Forthtelling is recognizing and verbalizing the outcome following a particular course of action. This prophetic function of the Church is its Spirit inspired proclamation of the Gospel and the consequences of godly or ungodly direction in individuals or nations.

Balaam, we recall, had a donkey advise him. But the more important record of Balaam is his refusal to curse Israel. His record portrays him is as forthteller, blessing Israel in defiance of his sponsors. But the Spirit also inspired prophecy that he could not have seen: foretelling events, some of which would only be recognized later in the New Testament. Balaam was a soothsayer, not an Israelite, but one to whom the local kings, in this case the kings of Midian and Moab, sought for divine favours. King Balak of Moab, represented the nations who feared the Israelites, and asked Balaam to curse Israel for their destruction.

Balaam was willing to try for the reward offered, but in his preliminary contact with God, he was forbidden to do so. After some altercations, God allowed him to go but only to say what God commanded. This led to four oracles, Numbers 23:7–10, 18–24; 24:2–9 and 15–24, that Balaam gave Balak. The first three were not prophetic in the predictive sense, as Balaam, in direct affront to Balak blessed Israel. For the first two oracles, God met Balaam and "put a message in his mouth," signifying what Balaam should say. The third is introduced, 24:2, as "the Spirit of God came upon him," and he uttered Spirit inspired words designed to frustrate Barak's intentions.

However, in his fourth oracle, Balaam claimed to be "one whose eye sees clearly . . . who hears the words of God, who has knowledge from the Most High, who sees a vision from the Almighty," 24:15–16. Amazing words from a heathen soothsayer. His prediction of the destruction of the nations that oppose Israel is understandable, but his veiled prophetic view of Jesus Christ is clearly Spirit-inspired: "I see him, but not now; I behold him, but not near. A star will come out of Jacob; a sceptre will rise out of Israel," 24:17. I doubt Balaam knew Genesis 49:10.

Evangelicals and Charismatics generally agree that prophetic utterance is not generally dictated, but given in a way that incorporates the recipient's temperament and personality; as 2 Peter 1:21 states: "men spoke from God as they were *carried along* by the Holy Spirit" (my emphasis). Balaam's experience illustrates the developing picture of the Spirit's ministry in the desert wanderings of Israel, prefiguring incidents recurring later in the early days of the New Testament Church. The Holy Spirit was preparing those of later times, and in particular today's readers of the Bible, of his widening role in the ministry of God's people.

5

THE TIME
OF THE JUDGES

READ: Judges 16:1–31

The book of Judges is a counterpoint to the enthusiastic knowledge of God that characterised the book of Joshua. In Joshua, a clear knowledge of God and his requirements directed the actions and accomplishments of Israel. We have already noted the filling of Joshua by the Holy Spirit for leadership and the gift of wisdom—much needed in leading the unruly Israelites.

There were, of course, failures along the way, and Joshua's record does not shy away from them. Joshua was aware of Israel's future waywardness, and in the last chapter of his book, he predicted the nation's failure to remain faithful, despite the people's protestations to do so. In this, he anticipated the later cycles of apostasy, bondage and liberation, summarized in Judges 2:10–19. It is not hard for us to understand the transition from Joshua to Judges. When a generation considers God restrictive or irrelevant to life, the next generation may grow up with little or no knowledge of the faith. Western Christianity is currently experiencing this. But Judges reminds us that God still intervenes.

The judges ruled Israel for the next 350 years, until the institution of the monarchy under Samuel. The word "judge" can also mean leader. It is clear from the book of Judges that judges did more than judge; they also functioned as warriors, leading Israel in warfare during the cycles of apostasy. In spite of Israel's disobedience, the Holy Spirit intervened, enabling the judges to lead Israel to victory against her oppressors.

OTHNIEL, GIDEON AND JEPHTHAH

Many of these leaders were charismatic. "The Spirit of the LORD came upon" three of the judges prior to the mighty and erratic Samson. Reading the stories of these judges, was the coming of the Spirit on these men a once for life investment by the Spirit for leadership, or a one time empowering for battle? For many who had gone before, there is evidence that the former is true: recall Joseph, Moses and Joshua. The explanation given for Othniel suggests that the same was true for him.

Two references from Judges 3:9–11 indicate that God's Spirit invested Othniel for leadership. He became Israel's judge, a lifetime position requiring leadership, and Israel continued in peace for the length of Othniel's life. The same may not be true of Gideon and Jephthah. In both cases, the Holy Spirit empowered these men for a coming battle; there is no indication that the

40

empowering was investment for life. You can read their accounts in Judges 6:34 and 11:29.

The story of Jephthah is also intriguing, in that while he was under the influence of the Holy Spirit for battle, he made the unwise vow that eventually caused the death, or seclusion—we are not sure which—of his daughter. This denies any suggestion that the Spirit's wisdom was directing his thoughts in a more general way than for the impending battle, and is a reminder that the inner voice of the Spirit can be overridden or ignored. This difference between investment of the Spirit in a person for life, or an empowering for a specific challenge or both, is one that we will encounter again in the New Testament Church.

Samson

Samson's record is the most memorable as it shows many more references to the empowering work of the Holy Spirit than previous leaders. In addition, we will find an investment of God's Spirit in his life, in addition to a special empowering in challenging times. Yet, Samson's wild life leads many to question the value of the Holy Spirit's influence in his life; an extreme example of foolish decisions and actions undertaken despite the Spirit's indwelling. It is a reminder that however strong the Spirit's presence in our lives, it is no passport to perfection. In particular, an overpowering experience from the Holy Spirit may lead to an attitude of spiritual superiority over others—in direct defiance of the Christian virtue of empowerment for service.

Two texts give the impression that the Spirit was with Samson on an ongoing basis. The first is before his appointment as Judge and ruler in Israel where we read, "The Spirit of the Lord began to stir him while he was in Mahaneh Dan, between Zorah and Eshtaol." Judges 13:24–25. The second is following the hair-cutting episode when the Philistines bound him for the third time:

> Having put him to sleep on her lap, [Delilah] called a man to shave off the seven braids of his hair, and so began to subdue him. And his strength left him.
>
> Then she called, "Samson, the Philistines are upon you!"
>
> He awoke from his sleep and thought, "I'll go out as before and shake myself free." But he did not know that the LORD had left him. (Judges 16:19–20)

Several items need clarification from these instances in Samson's life. First, Samson was a Nazirite, called specifically to deliver the Israelites from the Philistine occupation. An angel had told his parents, "No razor may be used on his head, because the boy is to be a Nazirite, set apart to God from birth, and he will begin the deliverance of Israel from the hands of the Philistines," 13:5. The "stirring" by God's Spirit early in life may well have been the call upon his life as a Nazirite, a sign of which was hair uncut from birth.

Second, his strength was not in his uncut hair, but in the strength of the Spirit within him. Allowing his haircut indicated that Samson considered his strength was his own, no longer from the Spirit within. Forgetting the source of his strength, caused the Lord to leave him, and he was at the mercy of the Philistines.

Third, his ability to draw upon his strength up to this time—

often capriciously, see 14:5–6, 19 and 15:13–15—signified not only the continued investment of God's Spirit within, but also empowering for specific events indicated by the refrain: "The Spirit of the LORD came upon him in power."

Fourth, which we shall encounter again, is that the indwelling Spirit does not guarantee a perfect life. What it does signify is God's immense patience with our sinfulness. But Samson's case also indicates that there may come a time when a wilful defiance of God's Spirit may cause him to leave.

Finally, on occasions like this, it is reasonable to recognize actions of the Spirit of God even where unaccredited. Samson's humiliation was a result of the Spirit of the Lord leaving him. This implied work of the Spirit is also true of the return of his strength. Again, his new strength was not in his hair, but the new growth of his hair coincided with Samson's awakened recognition of his need. Then the Lord's Spirit returned in physical strength as Samson called on the Lord's strength for final revenge on the Philistines. This renewed strength brought down the Philistine temple and "killed many more when he died than while he lived," 16:28–30.

Although these men were committed to God, sometimes the culture of the time infiltrated their thinking and actions. "In those days Israel had no king; everyone did as he saw fit," Judges 17:6. Subsequent stories in Judges record the religious pluralism of those days. Similarly, the widespread evidence of the Spirit's involvement in the Church worldwide has not always influenced Christians into valid spiritual living as the examples of Jephthah and Samson foreshadowed.

6

THE FOUNDING
OF THE MONARCHY

READ: 1 Samuel 10:1–12; 13:5–14; 16:1–14

The period of the judges lasted for about 350 years before the monarchy. The phrase "In those days Israel had
no king" repeated four times in Judges 17:6, 18:1, 19:1,
21:25, stresses the lawlessness of the time; the first and the last
references adding the phrase "everyone did as he saw fit." Chapter 17 to the end of the book describes the spiritual and violent
anarchy that existed following the stories of Samson. The story of
Ruth takes place during this time, and the warnings given to her
to avoid danger, Ruth 2:8–9 and 22, give a further glimpse into the
conditions of the time.

As we turn to the First book of Samuel, the prophet Samuel
and his sons Joel and Abijah were the last judges of Israel, and

Samuel almost single-handedly drew Israel back into the worship of the Lord. His sons failed to follow Samuel's instructions and displeased the elders of Israel who consequently demanded "a king to lead us, such as all the other nations have," 1 Samuel 8:4–5. Following this demand, Samuel tried to make it clear that having no king was not Israel's problem. God was the King of Israel, a distinctive that set Israel apart from the surrounding nations. Despite Samuel's warnings, the people continued to demand a king, God acquiesced to their demands, and Samuel warned of the consequences, verses 6–21.

King Saul

God, through Samuel, appointed the first two kings of Israel, Saul and David. They both experienced the activity of the Holy Spirit. Saul's story commences in 1 Samuel 9:16 as the Lord instructed Samuel to anoint Saul as leader of Israel, and predicted that The Spirit of the Lord would come upon Saul in power and he would prophesy with a group of prophets:

> The Spirit of the Lord will come upon you in power, and you will prophesy with them; and you will be changed into a different person. Once these signs are fulfilled, do whatever your hand finds to do, for God is with you. (1 Samuel 10:6–7)

This happened as Samuel said, and is reminiscent of our review of the elders of Israel, including Eldad and Medad, prophesying as God's Spirit upon Moses was shared with them. As with that earlier occurrence, this prophesying was more an evidence of the Spirit's activity than a predictive event. It was a public event, verses 11–12, giving the people assurance of the special anointing on Saul for leadership by the Spirit of God.

Saul's first test of leadership came as the Ammonites besieged Ramoth-Gilead. In an approach reminiscent of Samson, the power of the Holy Spirit came upon Saul as he sliced up two oxen and called the fighting men to battle. Here we see the two patterns of the Spirit's involvement: one the Spirit's investment in Saul's life, previously observed in Samson's life, and second, the empowerment for a specific need. The continuing investment for leadership is confirmed as we note the Holy Spirit departing from Saul and reinvested in David as a replacement king in 1 Samuel 16:13–14.

After reading the latter of these two verses, you may be questioning why the Spirit of God left Saul if the Spirit's presence was an ongoing investment? To answer this, we need to review Saul's leadership to this time. Two occasions incurred Samuel's wrath and God's displeasure.

The first was Saul's reluctance to wait for Samuel to perform the necessary sacrifice before going into battle with the Philistines, recorded in 1 Samuel chapter 13. As the conditions for battle were deteriorating, Saul went ahead with the sacrifice himself. When Samuel arrived, he made it clear that Saul's excuse for initiating the sacrifice himself was a reason for his action, but insufficient justification. Saul's circumstances, however severe, were not an excuse for disobedience. This was a difficult lesson, for you may have noted that pressing circumstances frequently lead us to cut corners off God's requirements. Hear Saul's excuse: "I thought, 'Now the Philistines will come down against me at Gilgal, and I have not sought the LORD's favour.' So I felt compelled to offer the burnt offering," 1 Samuel 13:12.

The second incident, told in 1 Samuel chapter 15, showed more clearly Saul's fault lines in his attitude; it had dishonesty written all over it. In disobedience to Samuel's directive to destroy all the Amalekites and their cattle, Saul kept the cattle for himself and hid them. His greeting to Samuel was: "The LORD bless you! I have carried out the LORD's instructions," verse 13. Samuel gave his classic response: "What then is this bleating of sheep in my ears? What is this lowing of cattle that I hear?" verse 14. Saul's rationalization of his disobedience had a spiritual ring to it; he had kept the cattle for sacrifice to God. Samuel's answer cut across all Saul's deception, "To obey is better than sacrifice," and Samuel terminated Saul's kingship, verses 22–23. Saul's forced confession coupled with the request to Samuel, "I have sinned. But please honour me before the elders of my people and before Israel," verse 30, was indicative of his downfall. Saul was more concerned with reputation than repentance.

1 Samuel 16:14 may also have raised a second question for you: How can an evil spirit come from the Lord? Christian doctrine has always held that God is not the author or promoter of sin, so how can he be responsible for an evil spirit? The answer lies in the function of this particular spirit, not in the spirit's nature. The destroying angel that slew the firstborn of Egypt was an angel performing God's will, but the effect was evil to the Egyptians. Similarly, a spirit or angel from God, that recalled Saul's memory and troubled his conscience, appeared evil to him and prompted his subsequent reactions.

Despite all we have learned of Saul, the Holy Spirit came upon him in one last event, recorded in 1 Samuel 19:18–24. While pursuing David, Saul discovered his location, and sent soldiers to capture him. When they arrived at David's location, God's Spirit came upon the soldiers and they prophesied along with a local company of prophets led by Samuel. Further soldiers sent by Saul did the same. Finally, Saul himself came and began prophesying with the prophets. Like the incident following Saul's original anointing, the prophesying was not predictive; in this case, it was the Spirit's protective measure for David.

You may still have a further question: Why did God's Spirit invest in Saul's life if he was not destined to fulfil God's requirements and subsequently lost the kingship and the Holy Spirit? The selection of Judah for kingship reinforces the question. Judah would provide the kings of Israel and eventually the Messiah, King Jesus, Genesis 49:10. David came from Judah; Saul from Benjamin.

Scripture does not provide a direct answer to this dilemma, but it is instructive to consider the context. Recall that an earthly king was in opposition to God as Israel's king, 1 Samuel 10:17–19. The anointing of Saul and the Spirit coming upon him showed that God would support and not reject Israel, even though their desire for a king and the subsequent selection, verses 20–21, were not God's ideal. Furthermore, without both Samuel's and the Spirit's anointing, the choices and subsequent failure would not have been authentic. This may be an example of the proverbial warning: "Be careful what you pray for—you might receive it!"

King David

We have already noted that the Holy Spirit came upon David at his anointing as king, 1 Samuel 16:13–14. Clear evidence of this investment of the Holy Spirit in the life of David is contained in three significant Scriptures. First, considering the Holy Spirit left Saul because of his disobedience, it is reasonable to assume that the same might happen to David after his adultery with Bathsheba. David himself obviously feared the same as he prayed, "Do not cast me from your presence or take your Holy Spirit from me," Psalm 51:11. Second, David's confidence that the Holy Spirit was with him lasted until his death, and his last words included, "The Spirit of the LORD spoke through me; his word was on my tongue." 2 Samuel 23:2. Third, David was aware that the plans for the temple he passed to Solomon were those "that the Spirit had put in his mind," 1 Chronicles 28:12.

You may well ask why David did not suffer the same result as Saul after what appears a measurably greater sin. Psalm 51 shows that David's sin began to haunt him, gripping his heart and causing him to fret: "my sin is always before me." He became aware that his sin was not primarily against Bathsheba and her husband Uriah, but against God, confessing: "Against you, you only, have I sinned." His sin also brought about a consciousness of the sinfulness of his heart: "Surely I was sinful at birth, sinful from the time my mother conceived me." His repentance was genuine.

This certainly did not mean that genuine repentance from him and God's forgiveness for him was the end of the matter. As Nathan predicted, "The sword will never depart from your house . . ." 2 Samuel 12:11–12; the consequence of his sin was, rape, incest, murder, and rebellion within his family up to and beyond his death. Forgiveness did not mean that he "got away with it"; he did not avoid the consequences of his sin.

We noted earlier that the investment of the Holy Spirit in

our lives does not shield us from temptation or sin. In fact, experience shows that it may even lead us to a sense of superiority and initiate the fall that follows pride. In addition, David's experience also teaches us that the indwelling Spirit does not protect us from the consequences of our sin. Any avoidance of the consequences of sin we may receive is by the grace of God, as is the forgiveness of the sin that may have caused our difficulties.

The Scriptures contain no report of the Holy Spirit coming on the succeeding kings of Israel. Rather, we see a general decline commencing with Solomon, David's son, and the splitting of the nation after Solomon into the two nations of Judah in the south and Israel in the north. In spite of valiant efforts by one or two kings, the decline eventually resulted in the exile of the two nations; first Israel to Assyria and later Judah to Babylon. However, during that decline, the Spirit of God worked through the prophets he sent to Israel and Judah, to which we turn next.

7

The Prophets
and Priests

Read: 1 Kings 18:1–15; 2 Kings 2:1–18; Ezekiel 37:1–14

Before the founding of the monarchy, the leadership of the nation had been in the hands of the judges. These leaders also included the office of prophet directed by the Holy Spirit as we have noted previously. Recall Moses and Samuel whom God clearly used, both to tell forth God's pleasure and displeasure in response to Israel's behaviour, but also to foretell the outcomes of unknown events. Samuel was last in this line of judge-prophets.

During the Kings

With the advent of the monarchy, the prophets continued as a separate office. As the kings took over leadership of Israel, so the office of prophet became separate from the leader. Instead of the two offices of priests and prophets (or judges), there were now three: prophet, priest and king. The behaviour of most of the succeeding kings of Judah and Israel may well account for the absence of the Spirit indwelling them.

If this is so, you might well raise the chicken and egg question: Did the Spirit resist empowering them because he knew their future evil rule, or was the absence of the Spirit's influence a cause of their decline? Recalling the presence of the Holy Spirit does not preclude sin in our lives may partially answer the question. But we should also note that selection may also depend on God's foreknowledge of our behaviour, noting that this may not be an either/or situation, but both/and.

So the true prophets of Israel became the voice of the Spirit. "For prophecy never had its origin in the will of man, but men spoke from God as they were carried along by the Holy Spirit," 2 Peter 1:21. In fact, during the remaining years of the monarchy until the exiles, the prophets were often a lone voice calling Israel back to God. Thus, in our study of the prophets, we assume the investment of the Spirit in their lives. Beyond that, we note the miraculous empowerment of the Holy Spirit upon the courageous ministries of some of these prophets during the declining years of the kings. Recall again the punctuated charismatic ministry of the Holy Spirit through the Old Testament.

In this section, we note the charismatic activity of the Spirit in the lives of Elijah and Elisha, and later prophets before, during, and after the times of exile. During the evil reign of Ahab and his wife Jezebel, a low point in Israel's decline, the enabling manifestation of the Holy Spirit reappears in the charismatic ministry of Elijah and Elisha some 150 years after King David. The references to the Holy Spirit in relation to these two prophets are few: for Elijah, 1 Kings 18:12, and Elisha, 2 Kings 2:9–18. But the context shows not only that observers recognised the presence of the Holy Spirit in the lives of these men, but also that their miracles attest to it.

In the first reference, Obadiah, a servant of Ahab but fervent believer in the Lord, recognized the Spirit operating through Elijah. He was fearful that the Spirit would transport Elijah away before he could arrange a meeting between Elijah and Ahab. In the second reference, Elisha was aware of the Spirit working through Elijah, and sought the same for himself to enable him for his calling into ministry. In the same passage, the prophets who saw Elisha part waters of the Jordan River recognized the Spirit from Elijah now rested on Elisha. They were also aware of the Spirit empowerment of Elijah, triggering their vain hope that God's Spirit had deposited him somewhere accessible.

While the references to the Holy Spirit in relation to these two prophets are limited, the miraculous work they displayed is evidence of the empowering of the Spirit in their ministry. The following table listing the miraculous in the lives of these two men illustrates the point.

Action	Elijah	Elisha
Control of the elements	1 Kings 17:1 2 Kings 2:8	2 Kings 2:14 2 Kings 2:19–21
Raise from the Dead	1 Kings 17:17–23	2 Kings 4:32–35
Increase Food	1 Kings 17:14–16	2 Kings 4:3–6 2 Kings 4:42–44
Heal Sickness		2 Kings 5:8–14

Not only was the ministry of these men both miraculous and prophetic, the miracles in themselves were also prophetic as they prefigured the miracles performed by the Spirit-filled Messiah Jesus several hundred years later.

During this time, an unusual incident is recorded of a spirit sent from God to deceive a warring party. This is similar to, and helps shed light on, the episode of an "evil spirit from the LORD" that came upon King Saul. The story is reported twice, in 1 Kings chapter 22 and 2 Chronicles chapter 18. It is well worth reading either passage; they have some amusing exchanges. But the passage of relevance to us is 1 Kings 22:12–23. The prophet Micaiah sees a vision of the Lord commissioning a "lying" spirit to entice Ahab to his death by predicting victory in a forthcoming battle, but in which Israel was defeated. It is critical to note that this "lying" spirit and the earlier "evil" spirit that troubled Saul were created beings obeying the Lord to accomplish his purposes; they do not refer to God the Holy Spirit, the eternal third Person of the Trinity.

DURING THE EXILE AND RESTORATION

The historical books of the Old Testament close with Esther. The books preceding Esther, Ezra and Nehemiah, record the return of the exiles to the Land of Israel, after the defeat of the Babylonian empire by the Persians. Following the poetic books of Job through to the Song of Songs (often called the Song of Solomon, or Canticles), the Old Testament records the activity of the prophets. These prophets ministered to Israel and Judah before, during, and after the exile, bringing warning, comfort and direction at a time of critical national stress.

During this period, we read of the Holy Spirit's final Old Testament charismatic activity through the prophets sent by God to direct and comfort his people. The most obviously charismatic prophet of the exile period was Ezekiel, with about 25 direct references to the Holy Spirit in the book. Most references occur in chapters 1–3, 11, 36 and 37. In reading these chapters, we note the variety of images describing ways the Holy Spirit acted upon Ezekiel: carry, fall upon, come upon, lift up, speak, stand, talk, lead, and take up.

Much of the ministry of Ezekiel records him being taken up and deposited at scenes of God's choosing. Of particular importance to the people of Israel is the scene at which Ezekiel saw the Glory of God leave the temple. It happened in stages as Ezekiel prophesied the downfall of Jerusalem; see 10:4, 18 and 11:23, where the glory of God moved from the inner temple to the threshold, then above the temple, and eventually to the east of the city. But in 43:1–5, Ezekiel sees the Glory of the Lord return to the final temple.

Perhaps the best-known passage in Ezekiel is chapter 37, describing the Valley of Dry Bones, immortalized by the song of an unknown author, "Dem Bones." Here Ezekiel sees the dead bones, representing Israel scattered among the nations, given the promise they will come to life again. Of particular interest for us is the wordplay in this chapter, notably in verse 9. The Hebrew word for "wind" or "breath," *ruach*, is also the word for "spirit." It could equally well be translated: "Prophesy to the Spirit; prophesy, son of man, and say to [the Spirit], 'This is what the Sovereign LORD says: Come from the four winds, O Spirit, and breathe into these slain, that they may live.'"

Normally, the context leads translators to select the best interpretation. In this verse, either translation makes sense, as the Creator Spirit gives life. Note verse 14, where the NIV translators used the word "Spirit": "I will put my Spirit in you and you will live." Later, we will see the same wordplay used by Jesus in John chapter 3, where, like the Hebrew, the Greek word for "wind" and "spirit," *pneuma*, is the same. Ezekiel makes a further reference to the Holy Spirit predicting: "I will pour out my Spirit on the house of Israel, declares the Sovereign LORD,"—also yet unfulfilled—in 39:29, before his final reference of the Spirit showing Ezekiel the return of the glory of the Lord to the final temple, 43:5.

There is no direct reference to the investment of the Spirit in the life of Daniel. Evidence of the indwelling Spirit in Daniel is from those outside the Hebrew faith who knew him. They note on several occasions the "spirit of the holy gods" in him, 4:8, 9 and 18; 5:11 and 14. This observance by the Babylonians recognised God's Spirit in Daniel, using their plural form for God, *Elahon*, similar to the Plural Hebrew *Elohim*. Because of the Spirit in Daniel, he "was found to have a keen mind and knowledge and understanding, and also the ability to interpret dreams, explain riddles and solve difficult problems," 5:12 and displayed "exceptional qualities," 6:3. Recall similar qualities and references we encountered with Joseph.

The exile was the most critical time in Israel's Old Testament history. We noted previously that the Holy Spirit appears in his empowering form during adversity and challenge, and this time was no exception. All the prophets at the end of the Old Testament recorded the Spirit's message of both warning and comfort, from about 800 to 400 BC, covering the exile of both nations, of

Israel in 722 and Judah in 586 BC. Even though these exiles resulted from their unfaithfulness to God, the heaviest concentration of the Spirit's prophetic ministry surrounded them.

Nehemiah, later recalling the history of Israel during his sojourn in the country of exile, noted the Spirit of God spoke to Israel for instruction and warning, 9:20 and 30. Israel generally rejected the prophets' messages, and their warning of the national consequences of ignoring God's direction still holds true today. God deals with the nations of the world as he has in the past with the great empires of the Old Testament and Israel.

If, as some predict, the heaviest persecution of both Israel and Christianity may be in the near future, the outpouring of the Holy Spirit during the last century may be a prelude and preparation for it. We have learned that the Spirit will be most active in any future challenge facing God's people, "Even though I walk through the valley of the shadow of death, I will fear no evil, for you are with me; your rod and your staff, they comfort me," Psalm 23:4. While we are told to expect persecution, those belonging to Christ will be spared in any forthcoming judgment of God, 1 Thessalonians 5:9.

8

THE MESSIANIC PROPHECIES

READ: Isaiah 11:1–9; Joel 2:28–32

There is an old saying that history repeats itself, and those who do not learn from history will repeat its mistakes. This has proved true during earth's long history, and it was certainly true of the roller coaster experience of Israel's commitment to God. Therefore, it will be no surprise to learn that prophecy is also inclined to repeat itself, leading to the phenomenon known as the double fulfilment of prophecy.

Many predictions of Israel and Judah's exile during the seventh and sixth centuries BC were examples of prophecies that referred to events of the exile, but also to similar events in later history. The language of banishment and restoration often enlarges in scope that can only be fulfilled by a reign of full justice by God himself. For example, the theme of exile and return can frequently apply to the later dispersion of the Jews in AD 70, forty years after the crucifixion of Jesus and the establishment of Israel as the Jews' homeland in 1948.

These examples indicate the complexity of analyzing prophecy as even the prophets themselves had difficulty understanding it, 1 Peter 1:10–12. Likewise, in our time, we have difficulties understanding much end time prophecy. The Old Testament prophets saw the peaks of the great events to come, but could not always appreciate the time lapses between them, much as an observer can see the peaks of a distant mountain range but not see the valleys separating them.

ISAIAH

Isaiah was one such prophet. He lived after the earlier exile of the northern nation of Israel to Assyria in 722 BC, but before the exile of the southern nation of Judah to Babylon in 586 BC. He saw in prophetic vision the invasion of Judah by Assyria and the siege of Jerusalem, 8:7–8. Jerusalem was not defeated at that time, see the historical chapters 36 and 37; it was the Babylonians under Nebuchadnezzar who finally sacked Jerusalem and exiled the inhabitants.

Isaiah has many references to the Holy Spirit, not always in reference to people. Two interesting references imply the Spirit's creative work. When the wicked have been driven from the land, the Spirit will provide for the creatures and birds that inhabit the abandoned land, 34:16. In 32:15, the land awaits the coming of the Spirit who will give life and fertility to the land of deserts and fields. The same arrival of the Spirit will also bring justice, righteousness, peace, and confidence to his people.

In this latter context, we review the magnificent chapter 11, giving clear indication of a time when Messiah will bring justice and peace to the earth. Verses 1–3 give evidence of the identity and character of the Messiah; he would be a "shoot . . . from the stump of Jesse." Although the line of kings that came from David, Jesse's son, terminated at the exile, the physical line continued. This Messiah will be of the kingly line and guided by the "Spirit of the LORD [who] will rest on him." Christians believe this Messiah came as Jesus, the second person of the Trinity, at his first advent, and will return as King of the earth at his second.

The Spirit resting on him will provide a partnership between the Spirit and the Son, giving "the Spirit of wisdom and of understanding, the Spirit of counsel and of power, the Spirit of knowledge and of the fear of the LORD—and he will delight in the fear of the LORD." Note this last phrase shows the Spirit and the Son acting with the Father, their mission to show and instil reverence and respect for God throughout the earth. The rest of the chapter shows this Spirit-led Messiah bringing righteousness to the earth, peace to earth's wildlife, and drawing the remnant of Israel's people back to the land.

Clearly, Isaiah chapter 11 refers to a future time when God will end earth's history with destruction of the wicked and establishment of peace and justice. Further passages refer to the Spirit's work in bringing rest to the earth. But while 42:1–4 continues the theme of the Spirit resting upon "my servant, whom I uphold, my chosen one in whom I delight," and who "will bring justice to the nations," in this passage he is portrayed as humble and tender to the disadvantaged. Matthew confirmed that this passage referred to Jesus, Matthew, 12:15–21. In addition, speaking to Jacob (Israel or Jeshurun), Isaiah, speaking for the Lord says:

> I will pour out my Spirit on your offspring, and my blessing on your descendants. They will spring up like grass in a meadow, like poplar trees by flowing streams. One will say, "I belong to the LORD"; another will call himself by the name of Jacob; still another will write on his hand, "The LORD's," and will take the name Israel. (Isaiah 44:3–5)

Furthermore, the fear of the Lord on all men will be the Spirit's work:

> From the west, men will fear the name of the LORD, and from the rising of the sun, they will revere his glory. For he will come like a pent-up flood that the breath (or Spirit) of the LORD drives along. (Isaiah 59:19)

Simultaneously, God will implant his Word forever in Israel:

> "My Spirit, who is on you, and my words that I have put in your mouth will not depart from your mouth, or from the mouths of your children, or from the mouths of their descendants from this time on and forever," says the LORD. (Isaiah 59:21)

Yet Jesus, at his first advent, claimed many of these prophecies referred to himself. He claimed to be the one having the

Spirit on him from Isaiah 61:1–2, and repeated the words at his self-commissioning for ministry in Luke 4:17–19. He was the One sent to fulfill them by the Holy Spirit's anointing, Luke 4:21. But while repeating Isaiah 61:1–2, Jesus stopped short after the first line in verse 2, "to proclaim the year of the Lord's favour," leaving fulfilment of, "and the day of vengeance of our God," and the remainder of the chapter to some future date. In claiming the first part of the chapter, he implied he would eventually fulfil the remainder. Thus, Isaiah's prophecies refer not only to Christ's first coming as the suffering servant, 50:4–9 and chapter 53, in the power of the Spirit, but also the return of Jesus Christ at the end of the age with the Holy Spirit.

The tenderness of Jesus is reflected in the Holy Spirit, as Isaiah recalls Israel's rebellion and God's deliverance, 63:9–14. He tells of the Lord's distress and care for Israel, as "his presence saved them. In his love and mercy he redeemed them; he lifted them up and carried them all the days of old." But "they rebelled and grieved his Holy Spirit." Yet he "set his Holy Spirit among them," and "they were given rest by the Spirit of the Lord."

Other Prophets

A further handful of prophets were aware of God's Holy Spirit in the Life of Israel, past and future. Joel, in particular, saw the work of the Holy Spirit expanding to the infilling of all God's people. He saw the day when God would, "pour out my Spirit on all people. Your sons and daughters will prophesy, your old men will dream dreams, your young men will see visions. Even on my servants, both men and women, I will pour out my Spirit in those days," 2:28–29.

This was to be a major change in the investment of the Holy

Spirit in the lives of God's people. Hitherto, God's Spirit was among them, see Isaiah 63:11 and Haggai 2:5, expressly upon leadership and others selected for specific ministry. Now, Joel predicts, the Holy Spirit would indwell all God's people. Peter confirmed the fulfilment of this prophecy on the Day of Pentecost, following the filling of all the disciples by the Holy Spirit in Acts chapter 2:2–4. In verse 16, Peter says, "This is what was spoken by the prophet Joel," and then quotes Joel's complete prophecy in verses 17–21.

Micah preached to Israel, often called Samaria after its capital, and Jerusalem, the capital of the southern nation of Judah between 740 and 687 BC. He lived long enough to see part of his prophecies come true as Israel went into exile in 722 BC. It was the general attitude of false prophets to refuse bad news, generally predicting victory and prosperity, often in opposition to the true prophets, including Micah, who warned of the coming exile of Israel and Judah.

Read Micah 2:6–7, where the false prophets objected to the Spirit possibly being angry—he only does good things. Against this Micah claimed: "as for me, I am filled with power, with the Spirit of the LORD, and with justice and might," 3:8. Probably all prophets, even the false ones, believed this about themselves; recall the false prophets of Micaiah's time and Zedekiah's impudent remark to Micaiah, 1 Kings 22:24. "Which way did the [lying] spirit from the LORD go when he went from me to speak to you?"

Finally, Zechariah, who preached to Judah following the exile, gave prophecies of comfort and directed the exiles to return to Jerusalem. In particular, Zechariah reminded Zerubbabel, one of the leaders of the returning bands, that the re-establishment of Judah and the rebuilding of the Temple would be accomplished

"'Not by might nor by power, but by my Spirit,' says the Lord Almighty," 4:6. It was the same Spirit that had earlier sent God's Word and law to Israel, but "They made their hearts as hard as flint and would not listen . . . So the Lord Almighty was very angry," 7:12.

That same Spirit was now the driving constructive force behind the returning exiles. Israel was resettling the land, rebuilding Jerusalem and raising hopes for the future and their coming Messiah. It would be about 400 years before Jesus was born in Bethlehem, although the majority of the Jews of that time would reject and crucify him. But for those who believed, an age of renewal by the Spirit of God was about to begin, when the next wave of his charismatic work would signal Messiah's coming.

PART THREE

THE NEW TESTAMENT

9

Jesus' Birth and Preparation for Ministry

Read: Luke 1:5–45; 3:15–23; 4:1–21

As we turn from the Old to the New Testament, there are clear connections of the nature and work of the Holy Spirit from one to the other. The most obvious are Jesus' claim of anointing at the beginning of his ministry in Luke 4:18–21 in fulfilment of Isaiah 61:1–2, and the coming of the Holy Spirit on the gathered believers at Pentecost, Acts 2:4, predicted by Joel, 2:28–29. Later, we will note similar terminology, signs of the Spirit's activity, and transfer from person to person as found in the Old Testament.

The pre-eminent purpose of the Holy Spirit was, and still is, to glorify Jesus. The descent of the Spirit as a dove on Jesus was accompanied by the words of the Father, "You are my Son, whom I love; with you I am well pleased," Luke 3:22. Later Jesus tells his disciples, "He will bring glory to me by taking from what is mine and making it known to you," John 16:14. Furthermore, the gift of the Spirit to the disciples at Pentecost was that they might be witnesses of Jesus, Acts 1:8.

We will also find clear differences between the operation of the Spirit in the Old and New Testaments. The giving of the Holy Spirit in the Old was vocational: artisanship, leadership, prophecy, priesthood, and so on. In the New Testament, the idea of vocation is still important but changes in character. First, the entire Christian community receives the gift of the Holy Spirit, not just selected persons for service. Second, while specific gifting for service continues, the Spirit of God is given to all his people expressly to further the mission of Jesus.

Jesus' Birth

Emphasising the significance of Jesus' birth, a fresh outpouring of the Spirit upon several people at the birth of Jesus occurs before the Day of Pentecost. This outburst of Holy Spirit activity in the nativity passages is in sharp contrast to the silence of the previous 400 years. Both Matt. 1:18–20 and Luke 1:35 confirm the creative Holy Spirit conceiving the Child in Mary's womb. Luke recounts the angel's message to Mary, "The Holy Spirit will come upon you, and the power of the Most High will overshadow you," reminiscent of the Spirit "hovering" over the earth at creation. Luke records more of the Holy Spirit's activity during Jesus' life than the other Gospel writers, and later wrote the Acts of the Apostles, a record of the Spirit's work in the New Testament Church. Luke's

Gospel describes in detail the work of the Spirit in the lives of those surrounding Jesus' birth.

The Holy Spirit filled John, later known as John the Baptist, from birth, Luke 1:15. John's mother, Elizabeth, became filled with the Spirit on meeting the soon to be pregnant Mary who would bear Jesus, verses 41–44. Elizabeth's husband, the priest Zechariah, encountered the angel Gabriel in the temple, who told him of the future birth of his son, John. Both Zechariah and Elizabeth, like Abraham and Sarah before them, were childless and "well along in years," verses 7 and 18. Because he doubted Gabriel, Zechariah became mute until the birth of John, at which time, filled with the Spirit, he prophesied the salvation of Israel from her enemies and the role of John as a prophet, preparing the way of the Lord, verses 67–79.

Luke chapter 2, following the birth of Jesus, records Mary and Joseph presenting him in the temple according to the law, where they met Simeon, verses 25–35. As far as we know, Simeon was not a prophet, but a devout believer. Nonetheless, "moved by the Spirit, he went into the temple courts." Luke records that "the Holy Spirit was upon him. The Holy Spirit had revealed to him that he would not die before he had seen the Lord's Christ." Not only was his prophecy clear on the role of Jesus, "a light for revelation to the Gentiles and for glory to your people Israel," but also on the conflict he would cause, and an oblique reference to the crucifixion, "And a sword will pierce your (Mary's) own soul too." The Spirit's work through Simeon was perhaps a foreshadowing of the Spirit falling on the common people at the day of Pentecost.

Jesus' Preparation for Ministry

Except for one incident when Jesus was twelve years old, we are told nothing more about him until he was thirty, when a flurry of activity by the Holy Spirit prepared Jesus for ministry. This preparation had three stages: his baptism, temptation and commissioning. At each stage, the Holy Spirit was closely involved.

All the gospels record the coming of the Holy Spirit at Jesus' water baptism, Matthew 3:11–17, Mark 1:6–11, Luke 3:16–22, and John 1:29–34. In whatever way the Spirit was upon Jesus prior to his baptism—we have no record of it—the descent of the Holy Spirit in the form of a dove at this time signified two things. John's account in chapter 1 points out the descent of the Spirit identified Jesus as "the Lamb of God, who takes away the sin of the world!" verse 29, and in verse 33 signified Jesus would eventually be "he who will baptize with the Holy Spirit."

Both Matthew and Luke are more colourful in their description of John the Baptist's forecast of Jesus' future baptism of his followers, adding to John's words, "he will baptize you with the Holy Spirit and fire," in anticipation of the filling of the Spirit on the Day of Pentecost. John follows this by a description of Jesus' role in separating the wheat from the chaff—those destined for life and death, repeated in Matthew 3:11–12 and Luke 3:16–17.

While the experience of the Holy Spirit with Jesus so far was pleasant, what followed was not. Jesus now underwent the second part of his preparation for ministry: his trial by temptation. Luke points out that Jesus returned "full of the Holy Spirit," from the Jordan where he was baptised and was immediately "led by the Spirit in the desert," 4:1. Mark is more direct, saying, "the Spirit *sent* him out into the desert," 1:12 (my emphasis); literally, he was *cast out* into the desert by the Spirit.

There he endured forty days without food, and in this weakened state, the devil tempted him to short circuit, and eventually forgo his ministry by taking the easy way out. This was a moment of greatest crisis, for Jesus' surrender to Satan's call for worship would have disqualified him to be the Saviour of the world. But it was also the event of the greatest victory, for he was "tempted in every way, just as we are—yet was without sin," Hebrews 4:15. Following his temptation, Luke tells us, "Jesus returned to Galilee in the power of the Spirit," 4:14. Clearly, both investment of the Spirit in Jesus' life, and necessary empowerment for service are evident in this scriptural record.

The third event was Jesus' self-commissioning for service. Here, Jesus decisively claimed himself as the Messiah. He stood up in the synagogue, read the beginning of Isaiah chapter 61, and declared himself as its fulfilment, "Today this Scripture is fulfilled in your hearing," Luke 4:21. In claiming fulfilment of Isaiah 61:1, Jesus maintained not only the coming of the Spirit upon him as experienced at his baptism, but also that he was the Anointed One—Messiah and Christ—by the Holy Spirit.

We discussed at the beginning of the book that the designation Messiah (Hebrew) or Christ (Greek) mean the same thing: the Anointed One. Later, the disciples recognized the special anointing by the Holy Spirit on Jesus. They identified Jesus with the Anointed One, or Messiah of Psalm 2:2, "The kings of the earth take their stand and the rulers gather together against the Lord and against his Anointed One." They continued, "Indeed Herod and Pontius Pilate met together with the Gentiles and the people of Israel in this city to conspire against your holy servant

Jesus, whom you anointed," Acts 4:25–28.

Others were not so convinced. Those who knew him from childhood became angry at Jesus' claim to be the fulfilment of Isaiah's prophecy, 61:1–2, in Luke 4:17–21. They considered him blasphemous and attempted to kill him, verses 28–30. In this regard, Jesus words were prophetic: "No prophet is accepted in his hometown," verse 24. You may be aware of many called into service and anointed for power, but unrecognized by those closest to them. Yet, persecution did not dull the Spirit's influence in his life; Jesus was filled with "the Spirit without limit," John 3:34, and experienced full "joy through the Holy Spirit," Luke 10:21.

10

Jesus' Teaching on the Holy Spirit

READ: John 3:1–8; 14:15–27; 16:5–15

C hrist's experience with the filling and joy of the Holy Spirit gives us a glimpse of his humanity, and in doing so encourages us, who are also human, that we can have the same experience and joy. But it was not just his experience that has been recorded for us; Jesus also taught about the Holy Spirit. John provides much of this teaching in his Gospel, as the thinker-theologian of the Gospel writers' group. We will set his teaching in the threefold work of the Spirit we first encountered in Genesis: creation, conviction, and indwelling.

The Spirit's Creative Work

We have already noted the creative work of the Spirit in the birth of Jesus. But the New Testament is more concerned with spiritual re-creation. Jesus claims that life is to be found in the Spirit, John 6:63. In this context following the feeding of the five thousand, he is indicating spiritual life is of greater importance than physical needs. Jesus also raises spiritual life in John's Gospel chapter 3, where he expounds on being "born again." The creative work of the Spirit in the lives of those who "receive" Jesus is the new life in Christ created by the Spirit of God. Verses 5–7 provide a parallel between natural birth and birth in the Spirit, "born of water and the Spirit," the latter signified by the phrase, "you must be born again." Catholic sources maintain "water" in verse 5 refers to baptism that is necessary for salvation, but it is more likely the flesh-Spirit parallel in verse 6 suggests that "water" simply refers to the "breaking water" of natural birth.

Jesus goes on to use a similar wordplay that we saw in Ezekiel chapter 37. Those who are born (re-created) of the Spirit are a mystery to the natural person. Thus, Jesus uses the Greek word *pneuma,* meaning both "wind" and "spirit," to describe the spiritual person. While we are aware of the wind, we cannot know where the wind originates and where it is going. In the same way, the natural person senses the work of the Spirit but does not understand it.

The Spirit's Conviction and Witness

John records Jesus' teaching on the convicting work of the Holy Spirit, as a witness to the world. "When he comes, he will convict the world of guilt in regard to sin and righteousness and judgment," John 16:8. Sin here is not breaking the law—that has condemned us already—but unbelief in Jesus. This is in accord with Jesus' earlier claim, "whoever does not believe stands condemned already because he has not believed in the name of God's one and only Son," John 3:18.

As Jesus represents righteousness, so Satan "the prince of this world," symbolizes coming judgment. The acceptance of Jesus by the Father and the condemnation of Satan stand in a clarifying contrast that measures good and evil and the glory and penalty that goes with each. Those who believe in Jesus and accept his reconciling sacrifice enjoy the former. Those who do not are condemned with Satan. The Holy Spirit brings conviction of these things and is the force behind our own witness.

In this regard, the Holy Spirit is called the "Spirit of truth," John 14:17 and 16:13, who "will testify about me," 15:26. These words are a reminder that there is an absolute truth, just as there is an absolute God, in contrast to the post-modern claim that all truth is relative. In addition, Jesus refers to the Holy Spirit as the "Counselor" in 14:26 and 16:7. "Counselor" is also used to describe the "Spirit of truth" in 14:16–17 and 15:26. The name Counselor is a translation from the Greek word *parakletos* (often transliterated *paraklete*), meaning "the one called alongside."

We worship the same Spirit of truth. Jesus taught the Samaritan woman that time and place are irrelevant to true worship, John 4:23–24. The critical issues for worship are truthful hearts, real before him. And because God is Spirit, we may worship him in spirit—he is not located in any one place or time; any place or time is legitimate and encouraged for worship.

Jesus taught that part of the Spirit's witness would be speech necessary for defence under persecution, Matthew 10:19–20, Mark 13:11, Luke 12:11–12. When the Jews arrested Peter and John for healing the sick and preaching Jesus as the resurrection, Peter experienced fulfillment of this promise; before the Sanhedrin, he was filled with the Holy Spirit as he made his defence, Acts 4:8.

Perhaps the defining reference to the convicting work of the Spirit of truth is that no one calls Jesus "Lord" except by the Holy Spirit. Jesus raised the issue that David referred to the Christ, or Messiah, as "my Lord," even though he was David's descendent. He quoted David: "The LORD says to my Lord: 'Sit at my right hand until I make your enemies a footstool for your feet,'" Psalm 110:1, noting that David said this by the Spirit, Matthew 22:43, Mark 12:36. Paul confirmed in his first letter to the Corinthians "no one can say 'Jesus is Lord,' except by the Holy Spirit," 12:3. I doubt this means that just mouthing the words is impossible unless the Holy Spirit empowers it; they could be said parrot fashion, or in jest or sarcasm. The words said in realization of their truth are a revelation of the Holy Spirit to the individual.

The Indwelling Spirit

Jesus' teaching of the indwelling of the Holy Spirit is in the form of a promise of the coming gift of the Spirit on believers. All the gospel writers recall John's words that Jesus would baptize with the Holy Spirit, Matthew 3:11, Mark 1:8, Luke 3:16, John 1:33. Jesus himself indicated that the Holy Spirit would fall later on those who are thirsty and seek him, Luke 11:9–13 and John 7:37–39.

Jesus' Teaching on the Holy Spirit

John also recorded Jesus' words that he would ask the Father to send the Holy Spirit just as he had been sent from the Father, 14:16–17. Jesus' words are instructive: "he lives with you and will be in you." The disciples already knew the Holy Spirit provided external guidance. The idea that he would one day indwell them points to the Day of Pentecost. This promise gave comfort to the disciples, assuring them of God's presence after Jesus returned to the Father, 16:5–7.

John's final record of Jesus' promise occurs in 20:22. In a strange action, Jesus "breathed on them and said, 'Receive the Holy Spirit,'" his breath a symbol of the Holy Spirit. This was probably in anticipation of the actual infilling on the day of Pentecost, the breath of Christ signifying the Holy Spirit as necessary for service as breath is for life.

The Unforgivable Sin

One last note regarding the teaching of Jesus about the Holy Spirit is the much-maligned issue of blasphemy against the Holy Spirit. Two gospel writers refer to Jesus' teaching on this subject, and Matthew writes:

> And so I tell you, every sin and blasphemy will be forgiven men, but the blasphemy against the Spirit will not be forgiven. Anyone who speaks a word against the Son of Man will be forgiven, but anyone who speaks against the Holy Spirit will not be forgiven, either in this age or in the age to come. (Matthew 12:31–32, Mark 3:28–29, Luke 12:10)

Attributing the casting out of demons to Satan (Beelzebub), the prince of demons, rather than the Holy Spirit, was the basis of this blasphemy. The context ascribes this sin to the spiritual leaders of the day who adamantly rejected Jesus Christ as Messiah. Casting out demons was evidence of the power of light over darkness, but they remained defiant at the revelation of the power of God's Holy Spirit, making the sin unforgivable.

Often known as the unforgivable sin, many have used this text to justify their rejection of Jesus Christ, because having blasphemed in this way they consider they are lost forever anyway. Others have argued that worrying about having committed this sin is probably evidence they have not done so. The determined and settled rejection of the work of the Spirit underlies its unforgiveness.

HIS FINAL INSTRUCTIONS

Jesus' final instructions regarding the Holy Spirit are contained in an overlap at the end of Luke and the beginning of Acts. Jesus directed the disciples to wait for the promise of the Holy Spirit in Luke 24:46–49. Luke then begins the Acts of the Apostles with an expanded version of Christ's words in Acts 1:4–8, predicting the Spirit's work in commissioning the fledgling church.

It is difficult to imagine the Christian life without the presence of the Holy Spirit. The whole teaching of the empowering work of the Spirit promised by Jesus could not have been only for the first generation of believers. If that is so, it dismisses the Holy Spirit's charismatic work throughout the Old Testament and limits how much of Jesus' teaching on the Holy Spirit we can depend on. Rather like those who pick and choose what to believe about the Gospel record of Jesus, similar dismissal of his Holy Spirit teaching forfeits any comfort we derive from the Counselor. Under those conditions, can we be certain of anything from Scripture concerning the Holy Spirit?

11

THE PROMISE FULFILLED

READ: Acts 2:1–41

We noted previously that Jesus promised to send the Holy Spirit after he left the disciples. Luke recorded the final promise and instructions of Jesus and his ascension twice, at the end of Luke and the beginning of Acts. Jesus' death and resurrection occurred during the Passover and he ascended forty days after his resurrection, Acts 1:3. Jesus told the disciples to wait "a few days," verse 5, for the gift of the Holy Spirit. It was ten days later at the Feast of Pentecost—Pentecost occurred fifty days after Passover—that the Holy Spirit fell on the gathered believers recorded in Acts 2:1–4.

THE GIVING OF THE HOLY SPIRIT

The Acts of the Apostles records the work of the Spirit among believers in the New Testament Church. As we review Acts, it is helpful to make some comparisons with the Spirit's work in the Old Testament. In particular, we need to review the large variety of terms used to convey the ways in which the Holy Spirit connected with believers in both the Old and New Testaments.

The Greek version of the Old Testament, the Septuagint, lists over twenty ways in which the Holy Spirit connected with people. The most common, are "come (sometimes leap) upon," "lead," "rest upon," "fill," "give," and "clothe." The phrase "take up" has the second largest use, all occurring in Ezekiel as the Holy Spirit transported him at times to various geographical locations. This phrase is distinct to Ezekiel's ministry and therefore less relevant through the remainder of the Bible and for us.

Phrases used in the New Testament include "fill," "be upon," "baptise," "clothe," "receive," "come upon," "pour forth," "give," "fall upon," and "be full." Several terms are common to both Testaments, indicating continuity of the Spirit's activity from Old to New. However, the New Testament references show that many of these terms are interchangeable. This is evident from various references to the coming of the Holy Spirit in Acts 2:4, predicted in Matthew 3:11 and Acts 1:5, as "baptism" by the Holy Spirit.

Luke, in his gospel, recorded Jesus telling them to stay in the city until "*clothed* with power from on high," 24:49. Acts describes that event by the term "*come on*" in 1:8 and "*fill*" on the Day of Pentecost, 2:4. Peter's description of that event was that the Spirit was *poured out*, 2:33. Reporting the experience of those at the house of Cornelius, Peter explained they "*received* the Holy Spirit just as we have," 10:47. Later, Peter recalled Christ's promise they would be *baptized* with the Holy Spirit. Now "God *gave* [Cornelius' household] the same gift that he *gave* us," 11:16–17, as he referred back to the disciples' experience on day of Pentecost (all emphases mine).

Thus, the Gospels and Acts use seven terms to describe the initial event of the Spirit's investment in the lives of his people: "baptize," "pour out," "come upon," "fill," "receive," "give," and "clothe." The question arises: why so many terms to describe one event? It seems most likely that language is insufficient to describe the remarkable phenomenon of God, by his Spirit, taking up residence in human individuals. Thus these terms, plus many others found in Scripture describing the action of the Holy Spirit, can only collectively give some idea of this experience.

The manifestations that accompanied the initial outpouring in the upper room were not expected at every filling of the Holy Spirit. While some future occasions report the phenomenon of tongues, wind and fire never appear again in the biblical record. Perhaps angels accompanied the initial outpouring, for "he makes his angels winds, his servants flames of fire." Psalm 104:4 and Hebrews 1:7. So to expect a particular manifestation at every filling of the Holy Spirit rests on precarious ground.

The transfer of the Holy Spirit from person to person is also evident in both Testaments. In the Old we have already seen the transfer of the Spirit from Moses to Joshua and the 70 and from Elijah to Elisha. In the New Testament we note the transfer of the Spirit from Jesus to the disciples after the resurrection, John 20:22, from Ananias to Saul, Acts 9:17–18, and from Paul to the disciples at Ephesus, Acts 19:6. We even find the prophetic conferring of spiritual gifts by the laying on of hands, 1 Timothy 4:14. In addition, there are different modes of the Holy Spirit's work shown in both Testaments, where we find the initial infilling of the Holy

Spirit, as well as subsequent fillings of the same individuals by the Spirit at times of challenge. Finally, there are references to being continuously filled with the Holy Spirit. These we will examine in more detail later.

The giving of the Holy Spirit in both Testaments produced signs on many occasions. In the Old Testament, Moses' seventy elders and later King Saul prophesied. We noted prophetic speech by Balaam and the predictive record of the Prophets. In the New Testament Gospels, we read of the dove settling upon Jesus, and in Acts wind, fire and tongues at Pentecost, and other manifestations later. Although these signs were frequent in the New Testament Church, they varied in nature, and in Paul's case, none are recorded. Furthermore, there is no record of supernatural signs to those added to the Church in Acts 2:41 and 47. This is no proof of the absence of signs, but modern experience suggests that some had an initial experience while others did not.

Despite the many similarities of the Holy Spirit's operation in both Testaments, there are specific differences also. In the New Testament, the gift of the Holy Spirit was for all God's people, Acts 2:4, not selected ones for specific service. Nor do we read in the New Testament of the Holy Spirit departing as we noted in the Old from Saul and Samson and the temple in Jerusalem. The gift is permanent to the Church.

The Spirit's use of tongues is also a new departure in the New Testament. It is clear from Acts chapter 2 that these were human languages explaining to the many nationalities in Jerusalem what was happening. It was a clear reversal of the confounding of languages at Babel, Genesis 11:1–9, and a foretaste of the breaking down of barriers between people groups in Christ, Galatians 3:28.

All heard the "wonders of God" in their native languages, creating both confusion and scepticism, Acts 2:12–13.

PETER'S INTERPRETATION

Most of the remainder of Acts chapter 2 is a record of Peter's sermon explaining the meaning of this unusual event. The commotion was not a drunken party, verses 14–16, but a visitation from God. Peter quoted the prediction of this event from Joel 2:28–32, announcing the work of the Spirit among the common people: "I will pour out my Spirit on all people. Your sons and daughters will prophesy, your old men will dream dreams, your young men will see visions. Even on my servants, both men and women, I will pour out my Spirit in those days," Joel 2:28–29.

Peter recognized that the work of the Holy Spirit was to glorify Jesus the Messiah, advancing the cause of Christ, probably with Jesus' words from John 16:14 in mind. Peter proclaimed Jesus accredited by God through his miracles, crucified by those who witnessed them, but raised from the dead by God, Acts 2:22–24. Peter reinforced his message in verses 25–32, by quoting and explaining David's prophecy from Psalm 16:8–11 concerning the Messiah.

Peter went on to make his listeners aware that Jesus, who had received the Holy Spirit, was now "exalted to the right hand of God," and had now "poured out what you see and hear," Acts 2:33. For Peter this was evidence that "God has made this Jesus, whom you crucified, both Lord and Christ," verse 36. Jesus was not only their expected Messiah, but also the Lord of the Old Testament. Peter noted the work of the Holy Spirit to bring conviction predicted by Jesus. His listeners were so convicted they sought remedy from him, verse 37. Peter's reply was threefold: repent, be baptised, and receive the Holy Spirit. The promise of this gift, evident to the onlookers, was for "you and your children and for all who are afar off—for all whom the Lord our God will call," verse 39.

Again, as we noted with Jesus' teaching, Peter saw the gift of the Spirit for those beyond his ministry, "for all whom the Lord our God will call." Those who were afar of in Peter's time were not only those geographically distant, but also those yet to be born. As God has called us into his family, the promise is for us also.

The coming of the Holy Spirit at Pentecost has a significant parallel to Jesus' baptism and the descent of the Holy Spirit upon him recorded in the gospels. Jesus, in Luke 4:18–21, claimed the anointing of the Spirit upon him was his commissioning to proclaim the gospel. Similarly, the coming of the Holy Spirit at Pentecost amounted to an announcement of the inauguration of the church age. The three thousand added to the church after Peter's Spirit inspired sermon adds credence to the meaning of both these events, as the Spirit inspired ministry of Jesus continued in the growing New Testament Church.

The descent of the Holy Spirit at Pentecost changed the disciples. Those who had been fearful of the authorities and despondent over the crucifixion now confidently proclaimed the Gospel. Peter's sermon on the day of Pentecost is typical, as the disciples preached the Gospel in Jerusalem and in missionary journeys to the world through the remaining chapters of Acts. Even under persecution, the Holy Spirit brought boldness and joy, 4:31 and 13:52.

12

The Gift Spreads

Read: Acts 8:14–18; 10:30–48; 19:1–7

As we noted previously, the Holy Spirit came upon the disciples on subsequent occasions after the initial infilling; the continuous residence of the Holy Spirit after Pentecost was followed by further independent occasions of filling by the Holy Spirit. Here we concentrate on the initial filling of others following the day of Pentecost. There are four specific references in Acts to these events. Each event confirmed the extension of the Gospel and its benefits to those the disciples may have considered ineligible by race or deficient belief. Recall that during their training, Jesus had told them not to go "among the Gentiles or enter any town of the Samaritans. Go rather to the lost sheep of Israel," Matthew 10:5–6.

THE HOLY SPIRIT GIVEN
TO THE SAMARITANS

The Samaritans were a despised group to the Jews. At the exile, the northern nation of Israel had been partially depopulated and repopulated with Assyrians brought in to mix with the Israelites. As a result, the northern nation, often called Samaria after its capital city, became a mixed race—the Samaritans—no longer "true" Israelites. Acts chapter 8 records the persecution of new believers by Saul (later Paul the apostle), which scattered believers; some to Samaria where Philip proclaimed Christ accompanied by an outbreak of miracles that authenticated his message.

Acts chapter 8 also recalls the Samaritans had believed and been baptised, verse 12, but the Holy Spirit had not yet come upon them, verse 16. Peter and John went to Samaria, presumably to confirm the Samaritan believers, and on arrival, "placed their hands upon them and they received the Holy Spirit," verse 17. No signs similar to those on the day of Pentecost are recorded, although there was sufficient reaction that the gift of the Holy Spirit was evident to Simon, verses 18–19. Clearly, the despised social status of the Samaritans did not preclude them from receiving God's gift.

THE HOLY SPIRIT GIVEN TO
PAUL AND THE GENTILES

Saul continued his mission of persecuting those of "The Way" by travelling to Damascus. Acts chapter 9 relates the story of Saul's conversion as the glorified Christ intercepted him, verses 3–6. Saul, blinded by the experience, was directed to the house of Ananias. There, Ananias placed his hands on Saul to be filled with the Holy Spirit, verses 17–19. At this event, there is no record of outward verbal signs, only his sight restored. Subsequent events and his later writings proved Saul's filling with the Spirit, as we shall see later.

If it was surprising that salvation came to the Samaritans, it was unexpected that the Gentiles could receive it as well, especially the occupying Romans. Peter's rooftop altercation with God made it clear that Peter saw the Gentiles as unclean and unfit for the Gospel, Acts 10:9–15. The remainder of chapter 10 narrates the story of Peter's visit, directed by the Spirit, verse 19, to the house of Cornelius, a Roman centurion.

Peter preached Jesus' death and resurrection, and, "While Peter was still speaking these words, the Holy Spirit came on all who heard the message," verse 44. The other believers with Peter were astonished, as they heard the Gentiles exalting God in other tongues. Peter was convinced; "Can anyone keep these people from being baptized with water? They have received the Holy Spirit just as we have," verse 47. Here was evidence of God's inclusion of Roman Gentiles in the faith and sign of their initial incorporation into the Church of Jesus Christ.

THE HOLY SPIRIT GIVEN
TO THE EPHESIANS

The final record of the Spirit's initial filling of believers is at Ephesus, Acts 19:1–7. Many there were already considered disciples, but their knowledge was deficient, having only understood the need of baptism for repentance preached by John. However, John's repentance was a precursor; "He told the people to believe in the one coming after him, that is Jesus," verse 4. Repentance was indeed necessary, but to be baptised into the fullness of salvation in Christ was a far greater inheritance. It was following rebaptism "into the name of the Lord Jesus," that Paul laid hands on them and signs of tongues and prophecy followed the infilling of the Spirit.

The gift of the Holy Spirit to peoples other than the Israelites, confirmed to the Jewish followers of Christ that their Messiah and his sacrifice for forgiveness and reconciliation was for all people. Peter had already voiced this fact on the day of Pentecost, recalling the promise to Abraham that through his offspring all peoples on earth would be blessed. But Peter understood this to mean the primary recipients of the Gospel were the Jews, Acts 3:25–26. These manifestations of the Holy Spirit confirmed that both the gift of salvation and the indwelling Spirit were universal and demonstrated the Spirit's vocational purpose to glorify and witness to Jesus Christ among all people.

FILLING AND BEING FULL

We have discussed the initial filling by the Holy Spirit of the disciples on the day of Pentecost, and subsequent initial filling of other groups, the Samaritans, the house of Cornelius and the Ephesians. This later filling of other groups recorded in Acts has been used by some Pentecostals as evidence that all Christians are eligible to receive the same filling after conversion. However, as we have suggested, it is more likely that those subsequent events were necessary to show the Jewish disciples that the Gospel was for all humankind irrespective of race or previous belief. Thus, the book of Acts describes the Spirit's initial filling of the Church worldwide as a one-time experience executed in stages to demonstrate the Spirit's acceptance of ostracised groups. The Scriptures are clear that "if anyone does not have the Spirit of Christ, he does not belong to Christ," Romans 8:9. After the original infilling of the Church in Acts, the Holy Spirit comes to indwell all Christians at conversion.

None of this precludes experiences similar to those at the original Pentecost, for Acts also describes further filling by the Holy Spirit of some disciples following their original experience. Typical is the description of Peter before the Sanhedrin, Acts 4:8; the fearful disciples, 4:31; Steven at his martyrdom, 7:55; Paul and Elymas, 13:9, and the dejected disciples, 13:52. As we have stated previously, the Holy Spirit provides specific empowerment at times of challenge. All of the experiences referred to, initial or subsequent, are described using the Greek aorist tense, which signifies a one point in time event. The widespread phenomenon of repeat experiences from the Holy Spirit in the Old Testament and in modern times is testimony to that truth.

But beyond these one-time experiences of the New Testament believers, Luke distinguishes between any one-time filling and being continuously full of the Holy Spirit. The use of "full" as an adjective in the original Greek designates the alternative idea of ongoing fullness of the Holy Spirit. This use of "full" as a continuous experience of the infilling of the Holy Spirit occurs in Acts 6:3, where selected deacons were required to be "full of the Spirit and wisdom." It is instructive to note the inclusion of wisdom, listed later as one of the gifts given by the Holy Spirit. Clearly, this is not conventional human wisdom, for the wisdom from God was "a stumbling block to the Jews and foolishness to the Gentiles," 1 Corinthians 1:23.

Chapters 6 and 7 of Acts follow the experience of one of these deacons, Stephen, who was not only full of the Spirit and faith, 6:5, but also "full of God's grace and power," sufficient for "great wonders and miracles," 6:8, and wisdom from the Spirit, 6:10. He declared the convicting work of the Spirit as he condemned the Jews for resisting the Holy Spirit, killing the prophets, and eventually betraying and murdering the promised Messiah, "the Righteous One," 7:51–52. Finally, Stephen had a fresh experience, "full of the Holy Spirit," which showed him a vision of "heaven open and the Son of Man standing at the right hand of God," 7:55. Here, Acts reverts to the aorist tense, indicating a special point in time empowering of Stephen as he faced the mob who martyred him.

The Ongoing Work of the Holy Spirit

Various aspects of the Spirit's activity illustrate the ongoing work of the Holy Spirit in the life of the Church and individual believers. Luke's narrative records the Holy Spirit providing conviction and prediction, together with guidance and strength at times of need. The initiatives of the Holy Spirit directed the building up of the Church, not only in Judea, but also through the first missionary journeys to various parts of the Roman Empire.

We have reviewed the work of the Holy Spirit in the Old Testament as a moral agent, Genesis. 6:3, and the teaching of Jesus regarding the convicting work of the Holy Spirit in John 16:8–11. This work of the Spirit continues through Acts, dealing with Christians and non-Christians alike. Luke describes how the Jews listening to Peter's first sermon "were cut to the heart," Acts 2:37, and the Sanhedrin had no answer to Peter's Spirit-filled proclamation, 4:13–14.

We also noted in Acts the anger that erupted at Stephen's

accusation that Israel had always rejected the historic witness of the Holy Spirit, 7:51–53, and Peter's similar accusation had drawn the wrath of the Jewish authorities, 5:27–33. Paul recognized the work of the Holy Spirit to Israel's ancestors who would be "ever hearing but never understanding; . . . ever seeing but never perceiving," 28:25–28, as he quoted from Isaiah 6:9–10.

Conviction was not limited to non-believers. The story of Ananias and Sapphira, 5:1–11, is a warning that Christians also need to be wary of deceiving the Spirit. The sin of Ananias and Sapphira was not in withholding some of the money from the sale of property, but in claiming they had given all of it to the Church. After all, as Peter said, the money was at their disposal to do with as they wished. Their sin was deception.

The Holy Spirit has always been in the work of prophesying the future as a huge part of Scripture testifies. However, it is essential to distinguish between scriptural prophecy, which is part of the permanent biblical record for all people, and local prediction which is not Scripture, but given for guidance at a specific time or place. Prophets were part of the New Testament Church as they had been for Israel in the Old Testament. Prominent among these was Agabus, who predicted a severe famine through the Spirit, which enabled the believers to prepare and provide relief where needed, 11:27–30. Paul, who was eventually arrested and shipped to Rome, claimed that "compelled by the Spirit, I am going to Jerusalem not knowing what will happen to me there. I only know that in every city the Holy Spirit warns me that prison and hardships are facing me," 20:22–23. It was Agabus who confirmed this prediction to Paul and the local disciples, 21:10–11.

The guidance of the Holy Spirit formed an important part

of the new Church's experience, essential to direct the leadership in ways not natural to human reasoning. The extension of the Gospel to the Samaritans and Gentiles illustrates the point. Several incidents demonstrate the Spirit's initiative in providing direction. We previously noted that Peter needed convincing that the Gentiles were not "unclean" people, and to go with the Roman Centurion, Cornelius, to his home. In Acts 13:1–3, the Holy Spirit directed the first missionary journey by Paul and Barnabas. The Spirit intervened in the second missionary journey Paul and his companions planned, diverting them to Macedonia, 16:6–10. We noted the work of the Spirit in directing Paul to Jerusalem and on to Rome, in spite of the persecution awaiting him.

When it came to disagreement among members of the early Church, Acts 15 records the discussion at the Jerusalem Council on whether Gentile believers should be circumcised. The apostles and elders that met eventually came to an agreement that "seemed good to the Holy Spirit and to us," verse 28. The Holy Spirit not only guided individuals, but was also interested in guidance of the corporate Church.

Acts chapter 8 records an enigmatic incident about Philip, one of the deacons chosen in Acts 6:5 with Stephen. The Spirit directed Philip to go to the Gaza road near Jerusalem, verses 26–29, to talk with an Ethiopian eunuch who was reading Isaiah chapter 53, but could not understand it. The salvation and subsequent baptism of this man, an influential official of the country, began the evangelization of Ethiopia. Then, verse 39 indicates "the Spirit of the Lord took [Philip] away" to Azotus, modern day Ashdod. Was this a bodily transportation such as we read about Ezekiel and Elijah, or simply further direction given to Philip?

Either way, the direction of the Holy Spirit clearly sent Philip to a place he would not have naturally considered.

This wide-ranging ministry of the Holy Spirit was the strength that enabled this small new Church. While specific incidents recorded are few, the gifts of the Holy Spirit were an ongoing source of strength and encouragement to the new believers. Typical of the Spirit was the encouragement of the Church following the first persecution, Acts 9:31, resulting in its continued growth.

13
Paul and the
Spiritual Gifts

Read: 1 Corinthians 12:1–31; 14:1–40

P aul's letters differ from Luke's strong charismatic theology by concentrating on the saving work and the day-to-day operation of the Holy Spirit in the life of the believer. In this way, his letters complement Luke's Gospel and Acts. Although Charismatics tend to rely on Acts to justify their beliefs and practice, they also place great emphasis on chapters 12 to 14 of first Corinthians. Charismatics claim these chapters are definitive teaching for their use of spiritual gifts in corporate worship. But Evangelicals point to these chapters as correcting excessive behaviour in the Corinthian Church, and limiting the use of verbal gifts in worship. Thus, a brief overview of these three chapters is necessary.

The purpose of these chapters is stated in verse 1: "Now about spiritual gifts, brothers, I do not want you to be ignorant." That ignorance, together with excessive enthusiasm, had led the Corinthians into arrogant pride assuming ownership of the gifts, 4:7–8, making it clear that Paul's teaching is indeed corrective, yet clearly not prohibitive.

1 Corinthians Chapter 12

The purpose of spiritual gifts is twofold. Jesus declared the gift of the Holy Spirit for witness to him: "But you will receive power when the Holy Spirit comes on you; and you will be my witnesses in Jerusalem, and in all Judea and Samaria, and to the ends of the earth," Acts 1:8. On the day of Pentecost, the gift of tongues did exactly that, Acts 2:5–11. Furthermore, the gifts are for building up the Body of Christ, 1 Corinthians 12:7, "for the common good." The Holy Spirit distributes them as he determines, verse 11.

The New Testament lists spiritual gifts twice in chapter 12; in verses 8–10 and 28–30. Other gifts listed in Romans 12:6–8 follow a call to sacrifice and humility, verses 1–3. Without these attitudes, the use of the gifts becomes self-serving and ineffective for the Spirit's work. Further gifts are listed in Ephesians 4:11. The lists given in the chart below show both repetition and diversity, suggesting the lists are typical, not exhaustive; other gifts are presumably available from the Spirit, but not listed.

Romans 12:6–8	1 Corinthians 12:8–10	1 Corinthians 12:28–30	Ephesians 4:11
Prophecy	Wisdom	Apostles	Apostles
Serving	Knowledge	Prophets	Prophets
Teaching	Faith	Teachers	Evangelists
Encouraging	Gifts of healing	Workers of miracles	Pastors
Contributing	Miraculous powers	Gifts of healing	Teachers
Leadership	Prophecy	Ability to help others	
Showing mercy	Discerning spirits	Administration	
	Tongues	Tongues	
	Interpretation		

Unfortunately, then as now, the gifts were often used for personal aggrandizement, creating two levels of believers; those who had the gifts and those who did not. This referred notably to the "visible" gifts, misused to dominate and manipulate those of apparently lesser spiritual stature. That, together with personal interpretations of life based on experience or personal "revelation" rather than Scripture, has led to disaster, as the story of Jonestown shows. Paul combats this inversion of spirituality through the remainder of chapter 12, by showing that members of the Body of Christ are similar to members of a physical body, each part equally dependent on the remainder. The less comely parts—probably referring to those who appear less spiritual due to a quieter disposition or personal handicaps—require special honour or care, verses 22–24.

Chapter 13 is the meat in the sandwich, clarifying that the gifts of the Holy Spirit are meaningless without love, verses 1–3. Paul selects the most controversial of the gifts, tongues "of men and of angels," and prophecy that "can fathom all knowledge," as hollow if not used in love. Even faith and good works are empty if not motivated by love. Paul concludes the chapter with the well-known verse, "And now these three remain: faith, hope and love. But the greatest of these is love."

1 CORINTHIANS CHAPTER 14

As Paul begins chapter 14, he reiterates the need for love to be the motivating factor in the operation of spiritual gifts. Then he refers again to tongues and prophecy, clearly stating the preference for prophecy over tongues in corporate worship, simply because it is intelligible. He takes the first twelve verses of the chapter to emphasize his choice, and closes verse 12 with the reason for his choice: "Since you are eager to have spiritual gifts, try to excel in gifts *that build up the Church*" (my emphasis).

The rest of the chapter, for the most part, continues his clarification on these two gifts, preferring prophecy but not prohibiting tongues, verse 39. Tongues are for unbelievers, verse 22, as demonstrated on the day of Pentecost and should be limited in the local church, verses 27–28. But even prophetic utterance should be limited, and the message weighed carefully by the listeners, verse 29, for the gifts are subject to the recipients, verse 32. Above all, Paul points out those gifts are for the strengthening of the church, verse 26, and finally, the Holy Spirit brings order not confusion, verse 40.

Paul's discussion of spiritual gifts in these three chapters raises the spectre of faking the gifts. Paul was not only aware of this possibility, but encountered it in the Corinthian church, and writes chapters 11 and 12 of his second letter to the Corinthians to combat the issue. In verses 1–6 of chapter 11, he attacks the self-proclaimed "super-apostles" in the Corinthian Church who had been preaching another gospel by another spirit. Those who considered themselves then and those who today consider themselves "super-spiritual" with a direct line to God through the Spirit are an easy target for Satan to deceive. This deception may take the form of other spirits informing them, or by simply assuming and claiming their own thoughts Spirit-inspired.

The purpose of God's intervention in human affairs is to accomplish a task that is impossible by natural means. The operation of spiritual gifts is a miraculous intervention by the Spirit for a specific purpose. An individual who has received a spiritual gift does not have it for unfettered use, but is a selected channel through whom the Holy Spirit operates. Spiritual gifts overcome human limitations and as such are miraculous and not exercised to order. However, the operation of that gift is under human control, 1 Corinthians 14:32, assuring orderly expression of the gifts. The Spirit's use of gifts in this way may be frequent or infrequent in any church at any time, but to speak as God's voice is a solemn charge not to be undertaken lightly, however exhilarating it may be. In particular, their use to proclaim the Gospel of Jesus Christ is paramount, Romans 15:18–19.

Evangelical suspicion of Charismatic prophecy comes from Hebrews 1:1–2: "In the past God spoke to our forefathers through the prophets at many times and in various ways, but in these last days he has spoken to us by his Son." This suggests that God's self-revelation was complete in Christ, and no further prophecy is necessary. According to this idea, the apostles and prophets of the New Testament who were the foundation of the Church, Ephesians 2:20 and 3:5, were no longer needed once the Church was established. Evangelicals and Charismatics agree that the Scriptures are complete, and no further universal prophecy can be added to them. However, the stories of Agabus previously referred to suggest the Church cannot lightly discount prophecy as unnecessary for specific and local needs.

NARRATIVE AS NORMAL PRACTISE

Some Evangelicals consider that only direct teaching passages, not narrative, are legitimate for instruction, and so dismiss much of the Spirit's recorded work in Scripture as invalid for today's ministry. They hold that experiences recorded in Acts are related only to the New Testament Church and are not normal practice. To the argument that "All Scripture is God-breathed and is useful for teaching, rebuking, correcting and training in righteousness," 2 Timothy 3:16, Evangelicals suggest narrative is acceptable for practice only where it is accompanied by specific teaching that supports it.

This begs the question whether narrative is limited to a one-time experience. There is no indication in Scripture that it should be regarded as such. If it were so, the historical passages in the Old Testament would have little significance for the Christian life, except as delightful stories of God's faithfullness to others. Furthermore, Paul has given clear teaching on the use of all gifts, including the most contentious, indicating the narrative gifts were normal operation in the early Church. Excessive enthusiasm for use of the gifts, especially prophecy, has often brought disrepute on the gifts, which Evangelicals have endeavoured to discredit by sidelining the Scriptures that express them. The extremes of Charismatic exuberance or Evangelical avoidance only further discredit the Spirit's work. If Charismatics wish to see the gifts given a meaningful place, their use must be discerned—using a much ignored spiritual gift—as genuine, and downplay the recipient. The use of the gifts must honour Christ and the Spirit that honours him. Each assembly has this responsibility to bring credit to the work of the Holy Spirit and honour to Christ.

14

PAUL AND THE HOLY SPIRIT

READ: Romans 8:1–17; 1 Corinthians 2:6–16; 2 Corinthians 3:7–18

We have already noted that Paul concentrates primarily on the saving work and day-to-day operation of the Holy Spirit in the life of the believer, although he takes space in 1 Corinthians chapters 12 to 14 to discuss spiritual gifts. Paul's references to the Holy Spirit are wide ranging, found in most of his letters. For convenience, we will consider his references under the headings already delineated in Genesis and elsewhere: creation, conviction and indwelling.

The Spirit's Creative Work

The creative work of the Spirit in the New Testament is mostly in re-creation of life by the new birth. Jesus himself tells us we are born of the Spirit," John 3:8, while Paul reminds us we are "a new creation" in Christ, 2 Corinthians 5:17. We are now "alive with Christ even when we were dead in transgressions," Ephesians 2:5, and our ongoing access to God is by the Spirit, verse 18. Paul confirms that we have become sons by God's Spirit, Galatians 4:6–7, even claiming we become "Jews," meaning part of God's family, by "circumcision of the heart, by the Spirit," Romans 2:28–29.

The creative work of the Spirit is not limited to giving us new life in Christ, but also in sanctifying us. The Galatian church clearly accepted the work of salvation by the Spirit, but tried to maintain God's favour by keeping the law, specifically by demanding circumcision of new Gentile converts. Paul forcefully reminded them that the gift of the Spirit was by faith, not by works, 3:3–5 and 14. We maintain our standing before God by the sanctifying work of the Spirit, Romans 15:16. We are both justified and sanctified by the Spirit of God, 1 Corinthians 6:11 and 2 Thessalonians 2:13.

The question arises, what does it mean to be sanctified? Is there a difference between salvation and sanctification? The New Testament recognizes our *position* as sanctified before God, but also being sanctified in *practice* as an ongoing process. For instance, the New Testament uses sanctification in the sense of salvation or justification in the opening verses in some apostles' letters; Paul in 1 Corinthians 1:2 (using the word "holy") and 1 Peter 1:2. Here sanctification is a status conferred on us. Compare this with the use of "holy" or "sanctified" in the Old Testament, where it meant set apart for service. That is our status within the family of God.

110

To be justified means to be "just-as-if-I'd never sinned." But while our perfection before God by the substitutionary sacrifice of Christ for us is our status, sanctification is also a process during our actual interim state, that of ongoing progress toward Christ's likeness. This is also the Spirit's work, "being transformed into his likeness with ever-increasing glory, which comes from the Lord, who is the Spirit," 2 Corinthians 3:18. Thus the Holy Spirit, who confirms our full sanctification, is also the source of power that guides us in daily life toward it. You may find the following alliteration is helpful. We have been saved from the *penalty* of sin. We are being saved from the *power* of sin. We will be saved from the *presence* of sin.

The work of the Spirit in our re-creation is full-orbed. Not only does he bring us new life and sanctify us, he also guarantees our final redemption. In Romans chapter 8, Paul reminds us that our assurance is not just faith in God's Word; that naming God as our Father is by the inward witness of the Spirit, verse 16. Furthermore, his indwelling presence is the assurance of the final redemption of our bodies, verse 23, when our transformation will be complete. This certain hope for the future is the Spirit's work, Romans 15:13, and Paul repeatedly claims the indwelling Spirit as the guarantor of our salvation, 2 Corinthians 1:22 and 5:5, Ephesians 1:13–14 and 4:30.

CONVICTION AND WITNESS OF THE HOLY SPIRIT

The convicting work of the Holy Spirit, first revealed in Genesis, is part of the Spirit's work in the New Testament. We have referred to Jesus' teaching of conviction by the Spirit in John chapter 16.

This certainly means cleansing and activating the conscience of the believer by continual warning of sinful behaviour. Conscience, unaided by the Holy Spirit and especially in unbelievers, is often unreliable due to distortion from the fall of humankind and also to the ongoing influence of demonic beings opposed to the Spirit, 1 Timothy 4:1.

The Holy Spirit is the One who not only inspires the Word to the authors of the Bible, but also the One who illumines the Word to the reader. Paul, in concert with other New Testament writers, recognized the prophets of earlier generations had limited insight into the mystery of the One who was to come. But the Spirit revealed to the apostles and prophets this mystery of Christ, Ephesians 3:4–5, who recorded it for our salvation. It is that same Spirit which now illumines the Word to us who believe and have the same Spirit, that we might understand the things of God, 1 Corinthians 2:7–14.

As noted in John chapter 16, the Holy Spirit is the One who convicts of sin. Paul confirms the power of the Spirit as the critical ingredient in his converts, so their faith "might not rest on men's wisdom, but on God's power," 1 Corinthians 2:4. Similarly, when writing to the Thessalonians, Paul reminds them that "our gospel came to you not simply with words, but also with power, with the Holy Spirit and deep conviction," 1 Thessalonians 1:5. It is encouraging to know that it is the Spirit's work to convince the unbeliever; our words and arguments are the opportunity, not the deciding factor in another's conversion.

However, the greatest form of witness is to the nature of God himself. God's people will reflect God's character; as Jesus said, "by their fruit you will recognize them." The greatest hindrance to the gospel is those who may proclaim the message correctly, even performing miracles, but the image projected is not God's, Matthew 7:15–23. Arrogance, self-righteousness, elitism, condescension, and outright condemnation are some attitudes that undermine the proclamation of the Gospel.

Paul lists the fruit of the Spirit in Galatians 5:22–23 using similar attitudes with which God described himself in Exodus 34:6–7 and Jesus used in the beatitudes to describe the spiritual person, Matthew 5:3–10. The following table compares these characteristics, with the opposites given in Galatians 5:19–21.

Exod. 34:6–7	Matt. 5:3–10	Gal. 5:22–23	Gal. 5:19–21
Compassionate	Poor in spirit	Love	Sexual Immorality
Gracious	Mourning (for sinfulness)	Joy	Impurity
Patient (long-suffering)	Meek (humble)	Peace	Debauchery
Loving	Hunger for righteousness	Patience	Idolatry
Faithful	Merciful	Kindness	Witchcraft
Forgiving	Pure in heart	Goodness	Hatred
Just	Peacemakers	Faithfulness	Jealousy
	The persecuted	Gentleness	Fits of rage
		Self-control	Discord
			Selfish ambition
			Dissensions
			Factions
			Envy
			Drunkenness
			Orgies etc.

The fruit of the Spirit, listed in Galatians 5:22–23, can also be viewed as an equation to illustrate how it functions:

Motive	Inward State	Outward Expression
Love +	Joy and Peace =	Patience
		Kindness
1 Corinthians 13	John 15:11 and 14:27	Goodness
		Faithfulness
		Gentleness
		Self-control

Paul himself exhibited attitudes of the Spirit in response to ministry hardship, 2 Corinthians 6:6. Furthermore, Paul worked toward the unity of the Church as he wrote his letters, noting in Ephesians chapter 4, that unity—even in disagreement—begins with the fruit of the Spirit, verse, 2, is a hallmark of the Spirit, verse 3, and all Christians believe in the one God, verses 4–6. Exhibiting the fruit of the Spirit is not legalism, Rom. 14:17; it is a natural outcome of the Spirit's activity in our lives, as fruit is natural to a tree. But it expresses itself in holiness, 1 Thessalonians. 4:8, and provides joy in suffering, 1 Thessalonians. 1:6

The Indwelling Spirit

That the Holy Spirit comes into the believer to dwell is not disputed. However, some Pentecostals hold that the Spirit does not indwell the believer at conversion, but comes in at a subsequent experience of baptism in the Holy Spirit. In response, Paul clearly states, "If anyone does not have the Spirit of Christ, he does not belong to Christ," Romans 8:9. Most Christians accept that since the day of Pentecost and other initial experiences in Acts previously discussed, the Spirit of God indwells the believer at conversion, whatever subsequent experiences may occur.

Paul goes on to confirm the indwelling Spirit of God in several Scriptures. The Holy Spirit is the gift from God, Romans 5:5, received in the believer by faith, Galatians 3:14, identifying us as sons of God, Galatians 4:6, and now as believers, the indwelling Spirit seals for us for the promised inheritance, Ephesians 1:13–14. This implies that without the indwelling Spirit, none of these is guaranteed.

Several times, Paul reminds us that we are the temple of the Holy Spirit. The inference in 1 Corinthians chapter 3, dealing with divisions in the church, is that the Body of Christ corporately is the Spirit's temple, verse 16 and confirmed in Ephesians 2:22. But Paul also indicates, in dealing with our sexuality, that our individual bodies are also the temple of the Holy Spirit, 1 Corinthians 6:19. When Paul writes that the Holy Spirit "lives in us," he is reminding Timothy that the same Spirit lives in all believers that comprise the Body of Christ, his Church, 2 Timothy 1:14.

If, as we have discussed, the Spirit indwells us, then we have a responsibility to live according to the Spirit. Paul discusses this at length in Romans chapter 8, where he refers to the Spirit thirteen times in the first seventeen verses, encouraging a "mindset" upon the Spirit and not the desires of our sinful nature, verse 5, for "the mind of sinful man is death, but the mind controlled by the Spirit is life and peace," verse 6. The passage indicates that we have a choice in the matter, verse 12, further pointed out in Galatians 6:8 and Ephesians 5:18. The chart below lists the effects of setting our mind on the sinful nature or the Spirit.

Mindset on the Sinful Nature	Mindset on the Spirit
What nature desires, 5	What the Spirit desires, 5
It brings death, 6	It brings life and peace, 6
Is hostile to God, 7	Spirit lives in you, 9
Cannot please God, 8	Spirit gives life, 11
You will die, 13	You will live, 13
	Children of God, 14–16

Our mindset on this issue determines the seriousness of our profession of faith. It is possible to reject the Spirit, grieving him, Ephesians 4:30, by ignoring scriptural injunctions or treating them with contempt, 1 Thessalonians 4:8. To maintain a mindset on the Spirit, we will strengthen our resolve and faith from the Word and by prayer, Ephesians 6:17–18, and develop a life of service "in the new way of the Spirit, and not in the old way of the written code," Romans 7:6.

In 2 Corinthians chapter 3, Paul points out that if the original written code, carved in stone, was given with much fanfare and glory, "will not the ministry of the Spirit be even more glorious?" verse 8. Life in the Spirit, when our mindset is on him is not a fading glory like our decaying bodies, but permanent freedom, verses 7–18, for we live in continuous fellowship with the Spirit, 2 Corinthians 13:14. Paul's Philippian letter, confirms this, 2:1, reminding us that our worship of Christ is also through the Spirit, 3:3, as Jesus himself had taught, John 4:23–24. Life in the Spirit is recognition of continuous investment by the Spirit, Ephesians 5:18

Living in the Spirit in this way is a two way street. The Holy Spirit responds to our commitment to him by providing strength, Ephesians 3:16, and help, Philippians 1:19. Paul wrote these letters from prison; his experience of the succour of the Spirit is authentic, and greater than most of us will ever require. In the middle of even the greatest difficulty, Paul reminds us that when we do not know how to pray or what to pray for, "the Spirit himself intercedes for us with groans that words cannot express. And he who searches our hearts knows the mind of the Spirit, because the Spirit intercedes for the saints in accordance with God's will," Rom. 8:26–27.

15

Hebrews to Revelation

Read: Hebrews 2:1–4; 6:1–8; 1 John 3:24 to 4:16

The remaining letters and Revelation in the New Testament, continue to acknowledge the work of the Holy Spirit. None of these specifically teaches about the Holy Spirit in the way Luke and Paul have, so their references to the Holy Spirit are more incidental to their particular message. Nonetheless, we can glean much from these letters and the concluding Revelation of Jesus Christ to John.

The Letter to the Hebrews

Following the letters of Paul, Hebrews, by an unknown author, heads the list of other letters: by James, Peter, John, Jude, and the Revelation of Jesus Christ, given to John during his banishment on the Isle of Patmos. Hebrews, as the name suggests, addressed the Jewish Diaspora of the New Testament time explaining how Jesus fulfilled the requirements of the law, in particular the Old Testament priestly and sacrificial systems, by his own sacrifice.

Much of Hebrews is stern, often reminding readers of the vacillating faithfulness of Israelite history. Most references to the Holy Spirit are warnings not to ignore him, and the references given increase in severity through the letter. In chapter 2, the author cautions his readers to pay careful attention to what they had learned, because "God also testified to it by signs, wonders and various miracles, and gifts of the Holy Spirit distributed according to his will," verse 4. He repeats the warning given to the Israelites in their desert wanderings, attributing the warning to the Holy Spirit, 3:7–11.

In 6:4–6 and 10:26–29, the writer is adamant that those that have known, yet insulted the Holy Spirit and rejected Christ's sacrifice for sin, would have no further recourse to repentance and could expect more severe treatment than those convicted under Moses' law. This hierarchy of guilt and punishment compares the lesser external cleansing by the blood of animals with the greater sacrifice of the "blood of Christ, who through the eternal Spirit offered himself unblemished to God, [to] cleanse our consciences from acts that lead to death, so that we may serve the living God!" 9:14.

THE LETTERS OF PETER AND JOHN

Peter, early in both his letters, recognizes the Spirit of God not only as the author of the Scriptures, but also the One proclaiming Jesus Christ through the apostles, 1 Peter 1:10–12 and 2 Peter 1:20–21. He goes on to claim in his first letter that Christ was "made alive by the Spirit," 3:18, and even the least violent persecution of the believer in Christ is evidence of the Spirit's presence upon him, 4:14.

John concentrates his teaching on the witness of the Holy Spirit in the believer in one passage in his first letter. Similar statements bracket the passage: we know the presence of God living in us by his Spirit, 3:24 and 4:13. The intervening verses in chapter 4 concentrate on recognizing false spirits. Those who recognize Jesus Christ as God in the flesh are from God, verse 2; those who dispute it are not of the Spirit of God. This sets the standard for assessing true Christianity from its devious copies. Furthermore, John makes the exclusive claim: "We are from God, and whoever knows God listens to us," verse 6. That verse recognizes the Holy Spirit as the Spirit of truth, thus the Word provided to us is authentic and secure.

We cannot leave John's first letter without comment on the reference to the Spirit in 5:6–8. A major variation between the New International Version of the Bible (NIV) and the King James Version (KJV) often creates both confusion and suspicion. The version in the KJV translates the Latin Vulgate, which includes a reference to the witness in heaven by the Father, Word and Spirit. No Greek manuscripts before the sixteenth century record this, and the NIV renders translation from earlier texts that exclude the reference. The original is clear. The three that authenticate Christ are water, signifying his baptism, his sacrificial blood, and the Holy Spirit, as previously listed in verse 6.

THE REVELATION OF JESUS CHRIST

John's first reference to the Spirit is the "seven spirits," in 1:4, also used in 3:1, 4:5, and 5:6. The NIV text note gives the alternative rendering, the "sevenfold Spirit." The seven spirits of God are evidently not the seven angels to the churches, as the seven stars, which represent seven angels, 1:20, are distinct from the seven spirits of God in 3:1. The phrase "seven spirits of God" or "sevenfold Spirit," almost certainly refers to the Holy Spirit for the following reasons.

The Old Testament gives some clues to this identification. The description of the Spirit listed in Isaiah 11:1–3, the Spirit of: the Lord, wisdom, understanding, counsel, power, knowledge, and fear of the Lord, suggest the sevenfold work of the Spirit. In Zechariah 4:1–6, the angel talking to Zechariah shows him seven lights supplied by seven channels of oil. The oil supplying the lights symbolizes the Spirit, who will provide power for the task ahead, verse 6. Revelation 5:6 repeats the idea of the seven eyes of the Lord given in Zechariah 4:10, which in both cases roam throughout the whole earth.

Finally, the sevenfold Spirit may also identify the Spirit's letters to the seven churches of Revelation, chapters 2 and 3. Following the message to each church, Jesus uses the identical phrase, "He who has an ear, let him hear what the Spirit says to the churches, 2:7, 11, 17, 29 and 3:6, 13, 22. Recalling the Holy Spirit as the Author of Scripture, the letters to the seven churches of Asia are also a call to the Church of Christ universal to adhere to Scripture. The Spirit of God gives messages of both comfort and censure in these letters and he is calling us all to hear his words; in the broader context, not only from the letters, but also in the whole of the Bible.

Other references to the Spirit include John's parallel experience to that of Ezekiel. In two events, the Spirit either gives a vision, or transports John to a place of vision, 1:10 and 4:2. On these occasions John claims to be "in the Spirit," suggesting a specific empowering referred to frequently in the earlier books of the New Testament. In the last chapter of Revelation, Jesus closes the revelation of himself to John with the promise of his return. In response, John places the Holy Spirit alongside the Church of Christ, the bride. Both with one voice say, "Come," 22:17, longing for the final consummation of all believers to their final destiny in the presence of their Lord and Saviour.

CONCLUSION

Apart from some Pentecostals, there is general agreement that the Holy Spirit indwells all Christians from conversion. The initial filling of the Holy Spirit to the Church occurred at Pentecost, but to ensure the apostles and new Jewish believers recognized the Gospel was universal, similar events occurred for disenfranchised groups: the Samaritans, the Romans under Cornelius, and the Ephesian "believers" whose teaching was deficient.

There are two types of infilling of the Holy Spirit apparent in Scripture. First is an initial infilling for the Spirit to take up permanent residence in the believer. Various signs may accompany this, as many references in both Testaments demonstrate. But the Spirit may frequently reside in a believer without an inaugural experience. There is no such experience recorded for Joseph and David in the Old Testament and Paul (called Saul) and possibly the deacons Philip and Stephen in the New. There is also no record of the 3,000 converted on the day of Pentecost receiving the Spirit with signs. Following the events of Pentecost the Spirit indwells all believers at conversion.

Second, there are visitations of the Spirit on individuals or groups on occasions of challenge or danger. These are point-in-time infillings that provide diversion, courage, speech or even a sense of joy in the event. In the Old Testament, the influence of the Spirit prevented King Saul from tracking David, and several judges had empowering episodes to defeat the Philistines. In the New Testament, Peter received courage and wisdom in response to the charges of the Sanhedrin, and persecuted believers experienced the Spirit's joy.

None of these examples replaces the work of the Spirit in unobserved ways in the lives of people. The Holy Spirit still guides through God's Word, spiritual wisdom, and inward prompting. Conviction of sinners would not be possible without the sovereign action of God the Holy Spirit. Descriptions of the ways in which the Spirit operated in the Bible do not limit him from other unrecorded methods of achieving his purposes. Conversely, neither do apparent evidences of the Spirit's activity guarantee it is the work of the Spirit; it is possible for impostors to reproduce many of the visible gifts of the Spirit. However, while different people receive specific gifts, the operation of those gifts is a miraculous intervention by the Holy Spirit, and do not occur to order.

Nevertheless, without clear direction in Scripture that the Holy Spirit's recorded actions were limited to scriptural times, it is presumptuous to deny his miraculous involvement in individuals and the life of the historical Church and today. The Spirit continues to work as Jesus did in the New Testament, particularly among the poor and disadvantaged in the southern hemisphere. Where much of the western church is affluent and apathetic, and where dabbling in prosperity issues and personality leadership dog the Christian ministry, I fear the Holy Spirit has retreated. Too often, attempts at replicating the charismatic work of the

Spirit result in "drumming up the Spirit," or spurious revelations and charades to manipulate others for personal ends.

However, the movement and empowering of the Spirit continues among the needy in all parts of the world, as well as those open to his ministry in the more affluent west. It is difficult to discount the experience of a quarter of the Church's two billion adherents as delusion, or consider them unorthodox when they align with Scripture and accept the Apostles' Creed.

Charismatic activity is a sovereign and miraculous move of God. But in more subtle ways, the Holy Spirit continues to guide and prompt as he illumines the Scriptures to us. We need to pray for power, guidance, and discernment in all events and areas of life as we experience the presence of God the Holy Spirit. But frequently a sense of failure and meaningless pervades the lives of devout western Christians resulting in lethargy and cultural conditioning. The antidote is the indwelling Holy Spirit who provides joy, meaning, and purpose. May we increase our hunger for the Holy Spirit's touch in our lives, perhaps as Tim Hughes seeks in his song *Consuming Fire*.

> *There must be more than this,*
> *Oh breath of God come breathe within.*
> *There must be more than this,*
> *Spirit of God we wait for you.*
> *Fill us anew we pray.*
> *Fill us anew we pray.*
>
> *Consuming Fire, fan into flame*
> *A passion for your name.*
> *Spirit of God, fall in this place.*

GONE WITH THE SPIRIT

Lord have your way.
Lord have your way with us.

Come like a rushing wind.
Fill us with power from on high.
Now set the captives free,
Leave us abandoned to your praise.
Lord let your glory fall.
Lord let your glory fall.

NOTES ON
FURTHER READING

This short list of books sheds light on various views of the Holy
Spirit, from conservative Evangelical to dedicated Charismatic.

Stott, John R. W. *Baptism and Fulness: The work of the Holy Spirit
today*. London: Intervarsity Press, Second edition 1975.
John Stott cautiously and compassionately defines the Evangelical position towards the Charismatic Movement.

Hamilton, Michael P., editor. *The Charismatic Movement*. Grand
Rapids, Michigan: Eerdmans, reprinted 1977.
A collection of essays analyzing the merits and dangers of
the Charismatic Movement from both sides of the issue.

Lancaster, John. The Spirit-filled Church: A Complete Handbook
for the Charismatic Church. Gospel Publishing House.
Springfield, Missouri 65802, 1975.
A measured description of the beliefs and operation of a
Holy Spirit filled church by a leader of the British Pente-
costal Movement.

Synan, Vinson. The Century of the Holy Spirit: 100 Years of Pentecostal and Charismatic Renewal. Nashville: Thomas Nelson, 2001.

A detailed history of Pentecostal and Charismatic movements from 1901 to 2001.

Stronstad, Roger. The Charismatic Theology of St. Luke. Peabody, Massachusetts: Hendrickson Publishers, Inc., 1984.

A scholarly thesis on the Charismatic material in Luke and Acts and its parallels in the Old Testament.

Green, Michael. I believe in the Holy Spirit. Grand Rapids, Michigan: William Eerdmans Publishing Company, 1975.

A charismatic Anglican's Scriptural understanding and experience of the work of the Holy Spirit.

ABOUT THE AUTHOR

Bryan Norford grew up in the UK, making architecture his first profession. With his wife Ann and young family, he immigrated to Canada in 1965 where he continued his architectural profession. Later he obtained a Master of Divinity degree at Regent College, Vancouver in 1982. He then pastored churches and taught in Bible colleges for several years in the lower mainland where he published a series of study guides on apologetics, ethics, and Bible surveys.

He is now retired and living in Lethbridge, Alberta where he and Ann authored their first book, *Happy Together, Daily Insights for Families from Scripture*, published in 2009. Bryan authored his second book, *Guess Who's Coming to Reign! Jesus Talks about His return,* in 2010 and continues to write. Further materials are on his website at www.norfords-writings.com. Ann and Bryan enjoy their writing activities, and spending time with their expanding family of grandchildren and great grandchildren.